"You're Not My Parent!"

Essential Tips on Surviving Step-Parenting and
Blended Families

Michele Sfakianos, RN, BSN

Open Pages Publishing, LLC
Estero, FL
http://www.openpagespublishing.com
(239) 229-2805

ISBN: (e) 978-1-7322722-3-1
ISBN: (sc) 978-1-7322722-9-3

Library of Congress Control Number: 2020918305

Because of the dynamic nature of the Internet, any Web addresses or links contained in this book may have changed since publication and may no longer be valid. The views expressed in this work are solely those of the author and do not necessarily reflect the views of the publisher, and the publisher hereby disclaims any responsibility for them.

Disclaimer

The information in this book is of a general nature and not intended to address the specific circumstances of a particular individual or entity. It is not gender specific; you will find instances where "he/him/his" is mentioned but it can also refer to "she/her". This book is written as a guide and is not intended to be a comprehensive tool, but is complete, accurate, or up to date at the time of writing. It is an information tool only and not intended to be used in place of a visit, consultation, or advice of a medical; legal or other type of professional. This book is not intended to serve as professional tax or legal advice (if you need specific advice, you should always consult a suitably qualified professional).

This book is dedicated to all those willing to step up to be a moral compass to children through step-parenting.

Acknowledgments

Thank you to everyone who has supported, not only "The 4-1-1" series, but the others book I have written.

Thank you also to my family for their love and support through this crazy process. My family has been a vital part and inspiration for writing the series. Providing the information to everyone, through our experiences, has been rewarding.

Thank you to my daughter Jenna for helping with the special section reviews.

Most of all I want to thank my step-parents for always being there for me.

Foreword

We all know the story of Cinderella. Fortunately, there was a happy ending but it did bring to light the "wicked stepmother." When it comes to step-parenting, the tale we should refer to is "The Tortoise and the Hare" – slow and steady wins the race.

Most everything you read about step-parenting has to do with evil stepmothers, obnoxious children, responsibility with no control, resentful ex-partners and lack of worth or appreciation. But do not be discouraged because there is a better side to step families. Step families, when working together, can work even better than several "real" families.

In 2020, approximately 39 percent of marriages will end in divorce and according to statistics and at least sixty-five percent would remarry. In my teens my parents divorced. When my father decided to remarry, it wasn't an easy adjustment. Seeing my father with someone else was difficult, but she helped to make the transition easier by not forcing a relationship. Fortunately, I had a positive experience with my stepmother over the years. Some people are not so lucky. Later, my mother remarried and again I was fortunate enough to get a great stepfather. Although divorce is hard on everyone, having a new step-parent doesn't have to be.

Step-parenting can be stressful and may be a difficult role to fulfill. Step-families, also referred to as blended families, are more of the norm now more than ever. When families "blend" to create step families, things rarely progress smoothly. A few children may resist the changes occurring, while parents may become frustrated or disappointed when the new family does not appear to function like their previous family.

Most changes to a family structure require adjustment time for everyone involved. With the right guidance and realistic expectations, most blended families are able to work out their growing pains and live together successfully. To create a healthy blended family, you need open communication, positive attitudes, mutual respect, and plenty of love and patience.

Contrary to what you may think, step-parenting is a two-person task.

This book is intended to share the trials and tribulations of my family and show you the outcome can be a great one. Life is what you make it, so make it great!

Table of Contents

Officially Dating

Coming Clean

When you find a person you care about, the one whom you would like to have a future with, you are going to want to bring your children into the picture. Of course, you want your significant other to already know you have children otherwise you may find a situation on your hands. Not every person is capable of accepting children belonging to another. A number of people are frightened of the responsibility children represent. There are women who are afraid of being called the wicked stepmother…and all it entails.

As soon as you are officially dating or can find an appropriate moment to mention it, you should get it out into the open. You don't want to get involved with a man or woman who has negative feelings about children. Most will have a reaction which may seem a bit odd, but it's not the same as having them say "I hate ankle biters" or call them "rug rats" and would never have them in their home.

Your children are going to figure out you have a relationship with someone—long before you are ready to bring everyone together for their initial "check-each-other-out" session. Older children will have the most difficulty welcoming a new person into their family. Children often prefer to have you all to themselves because of the memories of the life you had with their other parent. Even though the children know the relationship is over, it is still difficult to see you with another person.

Watch What You Risk

The risk you run with younger children is forming an immediate attachment. This is why you want to be sure your relationship has potential before you allow your younger children to bond. Even though you cannot always predict the outcome of a relationship, it is easier on a child not to have to experience unnecessary losses. Children may already feel a "loss" of one parent even though the parent is still in their life.

You also want to avoid including this new person in too many of your family days at first. You are beginning to develop a relationship which needs a baseline of a strong bond between you and your new partner. If your time is spent focused on becoming a family unit you are not going to be able to keep things in balance. You may be forced to skip a few important stages of your relationship on the course toward greater involvement and commitment. You are also trying to build a whole new family configuration as a single person with your kids. Your children, too, deserve your attention and your time while working through the change in their lives caused by divorce, separation or death.

You don't need to rush anything. You need to allow everyone to get to know each other and for you to decide whether you want to create a new family. If you have reservations you should listen to your intuition and wait until either the feelings are resolved or you understand clearly the relationship is not right for you. This is your chance at a new and happy life. If important aspects are missing, wait for another situation to come along. Don't settle because you are lonely or think you will never have the right opportunity. Don't try and force feelings that are simply not there.

Whether you are male or female, pay special attention to your children's reactions to your new love. Children often have their own way of sizing up a relationship, and may see something you do not but in fact, should.

If you are sure you have met the right person, give your children time to get to know him on their own terms. Give them space and do not insist on doing anything uncomfortable for them, such as hugging or giving goodbye or goodnight kisses, until ready.

If the kids are expressing distress, depression, resistance or rebellion, listen! Children need to have their feelings acknowledged. If kids see you are listening to their feelings, they feel able to listen to yours.

Remember to constantly reassure your children you still love them and no new relationship will change this love. Tell them you want to form a family and ask for their input. The more you include them, the less frightened children will feel. You may be surprised. If you have found the right person for you, your children may be as happy about them as you are.

Age Old Myths

Myths are beliefs. It is these beliefs which strongly influence the way people in step families adjust to their new family and react to one another. History and literature are filled with wicked stepmothers like the ones from Snow White and Cinderella.

Stepmothers in history are shown as wicked, cruel and uncaring. The wicked stepmothers steal the father's affection from the children, and have been known to take their inheritance, and out of jealousy make plans to have them killed. Stepfathers are portrayed as abusive. Stepfathers often complain people assume this stereotype and automatically view the relationship as a disaster waiting to happen.

Not all myths are negative though. The step-parent can be looked upon as a rescuer. You have the single parent currently struggling to make ends meet and then arrives a new partner to help. However, you have to be careful not to allow them to buy the affection of the children.

Step families have their own set of myths. First there is the "Brady Bunch" family. This is two families, each parent with children, coming together. If you buy into the "Brady Bunch" mythology you will either spend time in denial about the real, unsmiling state of affairs, or you will judge yourself too harshly for not being able to create a blended family free from problems. Second is the strange sort of family. Those in blended families think their family is abnormal or strange because it is "in-step" instead of their "real" family. Statistics show about half of all Americans are currently involved in a type of a step relationship. But, despite the facts, the mythology lives on, and as a result, step-parents often believe their families are not normal as compared to nuclear families.

Other myths:

Love occurs instantly
- This is the expectation: because you love your new partner you will automatically love his children; or the children will automatically love us because we are such nice people. Of course, if we think about it, we recognize establishing a relationship takes time. It does not happen overnight or by magic. Step family adjustment will be helped if we come into the relationship with our step children with minimal, and, more realistic, expectations about how the relationship will develop.

Adjustment occurs quickly
- People are optimistic and hopeful about remarriage. People want life to settle down and to get on with being happy. If your hope or expectation is once the wedding vows are spoken life will return to normal, you are going to be disappointed. It takes time for people to get to know each other, to create positive relationships, and to develop a family history. Just as with a new friend, work colleague, or neighbor, you can't expect a deep bond to develop between everyone overnight.

Children are forever damaged
- I can speak from experience here – I am not damaged! Neither are my children! Children go through a painful period of adjustment after a divorce or remarriage. Adults often respond to their children's pain with guilt. Parents feel the need to make it up to them. This leads to difficulties in responding

appropriately to our children's hurt and setting appropriate limits - an important part of parenting.

Children adjust more easily if biological fathers (or mothers) are not present

- Children will always have two biological parents, and will adjust better if they can access both. This means the children need to be able to see their nonresidential parent and to think highly of him. At times, visitation is painful for the nonresidential parent, but it is important to the child's adjustment and emotional health, except in those rare instances of parental abuse or neglect.

If the other parent dies it is easier on the children

- People need time to grieve the loss of a loved one, and a remarriage may reactivate unfinished feelings of grieving. These emotional issues may get played out in the new relationship with detrimental effects. When people remarry after the death of a spouse, their desire may be to want a relationship similar to the one before. When people remarry after a divorce, they are looking for a change. New partners may find themselves competing with a ghost.

There is only one acceptable family

- Today there are lots of diverse types of families; first marriage, single parent, foster, and step families to name a few. Each is valuable and has various characteristics. Because there are two adults in the step family does not mean it recreates a biological family. If this is what you are hoping for, you will be disappointed and frustrated when it does not happen.

Getting rid of the ingrained societal myths can be hard, so can giving up your hopes and expectations about what marriage, partnership, parenthood, and family life will be for you. The step family cannot function as the natural family did. It cannot and it will not. If you try to make it do so, you will set yourself up for failure. Also, you should not want it to. Obviously, things didn't work with the natural family, so why would you want to repeat those behaviors?

Be careful – these myths will set you up for failure:

- Remember the old cliché – you and me and baby makes three? What about his older brothers and sisters in the new family?
- I love kids and I am great with them. Do not fool yourself. Being a step-parent is unlike any other experience. You have a different role and more complications when involved with the child's parent.
- The kids will not be living with us so this will be easy. Again – don't fool yourself. What about summer vacation, holidays and other over-night sleep overs?

Myths are just MYTHS. Do not fall into the traps of them and do not give any more thought to them. After reading this book, you will find what works for you and your new family. Then you can laugh at the myths.

Before the "I Do's" Take Place

You and your significant other have committed to be with each other. You are in love, you are happy, and you are looking forward to a brand-new life. Do not automatically assume everyone shares your happiness. Chances are, at least your step children do not. But why wouldn't they? What may lie ahead can have the potential to be both a rewarding and a challenging experience. Know it can take a long time for a blended family to begin to feel comfortable and function as a family, so do not be disappointed if things don't come together immediately.

Consider the world from their point of view. For whatever reason, their biological mother and father are not together. This alone makes their world upside down. And now one of their parents has a new friend. With the possibility of a new adult coming into the household, children may feel threatened by your presence. The children may fear you will be taking their place in their parent's heart. They also fear you may be trying to replace their missing mother or father.

All of the above is enough to explain why your step children may not be friendly toward you and may even be outright rebellious. Your partner loves you, your step children may not. This is why it is important to start planning how a blended family will function before the "I Do's" take place.

First Things First

You have survived a painful separation, divorce or death of a loved one, and have managed to find a new loving relationship. Your first instinct can often be to rush into remarriage and a blended family without first laying solid ground. Make sure you give everyone a chance to get to know each other, and the idea of marriage.

- Make it clear you will not be put in a position to have to choose sides. Remind your partner and your children you want both sets of people in your life.
- Too many changes at one time can upset your children. Newly blended families will have the highest success rate if the couple waits at least two years or more after a divorce before marriage. Although this may sound like a long time, the more time you give the children to adjust the more accepting everyone will be.
- Make sure to experience the daily routine together before moving in. Spending time together at home and out in public will help build a bond. Although your first instinct is to take them to a theme park or other expensive type of outing, don't just do fun things because it is not a true test of reality. You cannot buy reality.
- Love and affection take time to develop. Get to know your partners children. Do not rush it. Do not try and force a relationship. Because you give time, energy, love, and affection to your new partner's kids you may not see the return immediately. Hang in there – it will happen.
- Have the discussion on how you intend to parent together. Make the necessary adjustments to your parenting styles before you remarry. It will make for a smoother transition and your kids will not be angry at your new spouse for making changes.
- Insist on respect. You can't insist people like each other but you can insist everyone treat one another with respect. This is one of the most important items.

If you give the right support, all children involved should gradually adjust to the reality of an upcoming marriage and being part of a new blended family.

To Have Success

Do not try to make a blended family an exact replica of your first family, or the idea of what you think is an ideal family, as this can cause confusion, frustration, and disappointment. Instead, embrace the differences and find ways to incorporate these suggestions:

- A solid marriage. Let's face it, without the marriage, there is no family. Most couples starting out have time alone however with a blended family marriage it is harder to have this time due to parenteral responsibilities. You will have to grow and mature into the marriage while parenting.
- Be nice. If family members can be tolerant of one another on a regular basis rather than ignoring, purposely trying to hurt each other, or withdrawing from each other, you are on the right track.
- Acknowledge each individual's level. Acknowledge each member in the blended family and what level each person may be at; such as teens versus toddlers or those at another level of acceptance of the marriage. Everyone needs to be acknowledged for their identity and respected for the level they are on.
- Don't show favoritism. We all want to be accepted, but showing favoritism of one child over another, just causes more issues.
- Give them time. After a few years of being blended, the family will grow and members will choose to spend more time together and feel closer to one another. Anyone with an insecure attachment history may have problems establishing close, loving

bonds with new members of a blended family. Fortunately, an insecurely attached child (or adult) can learn to trust others over time and bond with people who treat him with consistent affection, attention, and respect.

Each Child is Different

Children of various ages and genders will adjust differently to a blended family. The physical and emotional needs of a two-year-old girl are incomparable than those of a thirteen-year-old boy, but do not mistake differences in development and age for differences in fundamental needs. Because a teenager may take a long time accepting your love and affection doesn't mean she does not want it. You will need to adjust your approach with the various age levels and genders, but your goal of establishing a trusting relationship is the same.

Young children under 10
- Are more accepting of a new adult
- Will feel competitive for their parent's attention
- Have more daily basic needs to be met
- Thrive on family relationships

Adolescents aged 10-14
- May not be able to demonstrate their feelings openly but may be more in need of love, support, discipline and attention than those under 10.
- May have the most difficult time adjusting to a new step-parent.
- Will need more time to bond before accepting a new person in charge.

Teenagers 15 and older

- This is a time when teenagers tend to separate from the family and form their own identities.
- Teenagers may have less involvement in step family life.
- The most rebellious of all children.
- Teens need to know they are loved, supported and secure (from a distance).

No matter the age, the gender tendency appears to be:
- Both boys and girls in step families tend to prefer verbal affection, such as praises or compliments, rather than physical closeness, like hugs and kisses. Allow them to tell you their feelings and preferences.
- Girls tend to be uncomfortable with physical displays of affection from their stepfather.
- Girls tend to be more protective of their biological fathers.
- Boys seem to accept a stepfather more quickly than girls.
- Boys tend to be more protective of their biological mothers.

Blended Family Differences

There can and will be differences in blended families. Recognizing these differences ahead of time can help lead to a healthy blended family. Make it a priority to agree on consistent guidelines and strategies to show the kids you and your spouse intend to deal with issues in a similar way. This should diminish feelings of unfairness.

Common differences:

- Age differences. In blended families, there may be children with birthdays closer to one another than with natural siblings, or the

new step-parent may be only a few years older than the eldest
child.

- Being a new parent. One step-parent may have never been a
parent before and therefore may have no experience with the
stages children go through.
- New role insecurities. A step-parent may be anxious about how
she compares to a child's natural parent, or may grow resentful if
the step children compare them unfavorably to the natural
parent.
- Changes in family structure. If both parents remarry partners
with existing families, it can mean children now find themselves
with different roles in two blended families. For example, one
child may be the eldest in one step family but the youngest in the
other. Blending families may also mean one child loses her
uniqueness as the only girl in the family.
- Changes in family traditions. Most families have distinctive ideas
about how annual events such as holidays, birthdays, and family
vacations should be spent. Kids may feel resentful when forced
to go along with another persons' routine. Try to find common
ground or create new traditions for your blended family.
- Rejecting a new parent. If children have spent a long time in a
one-parent family, or if children still nurture hopes of
reconciling their parents, it may be difficult for them to accept a
new person.

If you had family routines in your prior marriage, make sure to consult
with the children before eliminating those routines. Discuss new things
of interest to both new families. Make new routines and new memories.
Suggest things such as weekend visits to the beach, a Wednesday family
night – perhaps playing video games together, or special ways to
celebrate family holidays. By bringing the family together to talk and

bond, and also by encouraging their participation, it will help to get them more comfortable with the relationship.

A family cannot be said to be truly blended until all members – both parents and children – fully accept one another as part of a family unit. Remember, be patient as this can take up to two years or more.

Relationship Building and Roles

Children, when they put their mind to it, can sabotage a relationship. This is all the more reason to take it slow when trying to build a relationship with them. Developing a positive relationship with your step children early on is the key. However, don't try and force the relationship. Make sure to address the immediate basic needs and your chances of success will be greater. Children want to feel:

- Safe and secure. Children want to be able to count on parents and step-parents.
- Love and attention. Kids like to see and feel your affection, although it should be a gradual process, not a forced one.
- Seen, Heard and Valued. Most children feel unimportant or invisible when it comes to decision making in the new blended family. Recognize their role in the family when you make decisions. Make sure to create an environment where the children can express their opinion without the fear of being judged or disciplined. Encourage their participation.
- Limits and boundaries. All children need limits and boundaries whether they think they do or not. Continued structure in a child's life is vital to their growth and development. New step-parents should not be the enforcer at first. There has to be a team effort when setting limits.
- Patience and Interest. Every child is unique and will show you how slow or fast to go as you get to know them. A number of children may be more open and willing to engage. Shy, introverted children may require you to slow down and give them more time to warm up to you. Given enough time,

patience, and interest, most children will eventually give you a chance.

Step-Parental Roles

It is only natural you would want your step children to love you, respect and obey you. It is also only natural you might feel you have no right to their love, respect or obedience. The only thing you may be certain of is you feel out of place and uncertain of what your role in this new family unit might be.

To know what your role should be you must first understand what your role is not. You are not your step child's mother or father, and you are not their friend. You may be stepping into a place in your partner's life once occupied by another. But you are not the other person. And you should not try to be. So, the first key to successful step-parenting is to be you.

You also want to avoid the pitfall of trying to be a friend to your step children. Children have plenty of friends, most likely, and you are not meant to be among those. Your first inclination might be to try to bribe them with gifts and kindness, to overlook bad behavior, and to try to be there for them. All you will win from this behavior, however, is a spoiled and manipulative step child.

If you cannot be your step child's mother or father or friend, then who are you supposed to be? The key is in the word step-parent. You are a parent. Your duty to your step children is to parent them. You provide a moral compass for them, you provide discipline as discussed by you and your partner, and you help your partner provide a home and sustenance for them. Be fair in all of the above, but also be firm and consistent. We will discuss "Discipline" in another chapter.

Be friendly but never let your kindness be motivated out of guilt or a desire to win over your step child. Children are evolving creatures that change over time. So do adults. You have to be consistent even when the rewards are small or missing.

One challenge to creating a cohesive blended family is establishing trust. The children may feel uncertain about their new family and resist your efforts to get to know them. Learn not to take their lack of enthusiasm (and other negative attitudes) personally. It is not as if the children don't want you to be happy. Kids don't know what it will be like to share their parent with a new spouse, let alone other children. These feelings are normal.

The stepmother or stepfather should actively support the child's relationship with the biological mother or father no longer in the home. For example, if you are in the role of stepfather, you should make it a priority to nurture a relationship between you and the biological father and to find every possible way you can to support a relationship between him and his children. By taking the high road of being the facilitator, you will find it easier to overcome feelings of resentment both on the part of the biological father and the children he no longer has daily access to. This may require a real internal commitment on your part, because supporting your step children's relationship with their biological, but absent, parent may seem small as to also supporting the parent's relationship with your spouse. Do not let jealousy or envy of the bond the parent shares with their children or the working relationship, and history with your current partner, be the cause of you being less than supportive of the relationship.

Part of your role as a new step-parent is to decide what you want to be called. Be careful when you take a title. You do not want a title of another person. It is easy to have a child under the age of two call you Mommy, however if the biological mother is in the picture, there may be resentment and hurt feelings. So be careful of the title you select. Discuss it with the children, if old enough to understand, provide options, and let them make the decision.

In time, if you parent your step children appropriately, you will find your relationship will grow and improve until the time the children reach a place where the distinction of step is not even necessary - for you or for them.

Part-Time Step-parenting

When there is shared or joint custody (custody discussed in another chapter), you can divide up the children's time in distinctive ways. You may get every other weekend and one night during the week; weekdays or weekends; or there are times when there is open time between homes, and the kids come and go. This works when the kids are older and ready to dictate their own schedules.

It is the fairest and most reasonable approach, both for the parents and the kids, if the children spend equal time in each house. But in other ways, it is more stressful for the children, especially if when shifting houses every week or more than once a week. When kids have two houses all the time, they can begin to feel confused and may never be sure of where they are or where they belong:

Be aware of this: If a child is in charge of when he goes where, he may use this freedom as a threat, or weapon against you. If you do not let him do as he pleases, he may tell you he is going to stay at the other parents' home more to guilt you into letting him do what he wants. Open houses only work when there is proper communication between the two biological parents.

Because the step children are with you half the time, you are definitely a part of their lives as a parental figure. Always make sure to welcome the children back into the home during visitation.

Successful Step-Parenting and Communication

I am not going to tell you everything is going to be great, wonderful and successful from the start. However, if you communicate often and openly with all parties involved, (partner, ex-partner and children) chances are the children will adjust better especially if aware they have access to both biological parents. It is important if all parents are involved and work toward a parenting partnership.

- Let the kids know you and your ex-spouse will continue to love them and be there for them throughout their lives.
- Tell the kids your new partner will not be a 'replacement' mom or dad, but another person to love and support them.
- The way a blended family communicates is an example of the level of trust between family members. When communication is clear, open, and frequent, there are fewer opportunities for misunderstandings and more possibilities for connections, whether it is between parent and child, step-parent and step child, or between step siblings.

Make sure to:

- Be yourself.
- Listen respectfully to one another.
- Address conflict positively.
- Establish an open and nonjudgmental atmosphere.
- Do things and go places together.
- Show affection to one another comfortably.
- Have respect for everyone's personal space.

- Be flexible.
- Shed anger and bitterness.
- Be honest.
- Be patient.
- Keep your sense of humor.
- Learn to compromise.

Learning to Communicate with Step Children

Soon after you move in, you will most likely face your first experience with step family conflict. You may feel resentful, the kids may feel rejected and furious, and your partner may feel caught in the middle. Resentments and resistance don't just fade away so you will want to incorporate active listening strategies.

Strategies to consider:

- Active listening helps the children by raising their sense of self-worth and self-respect. Whether or not your own child or your step child-to-be expresses it to you, your thoughts and your opinions of them matter. The fact you are listening to their concerns will help them feel better about you and your relationship.
- Active listening is a communication technique that requires the listener to understand, interpret, and evaluate what they hear. Once you hear the child's concerns, you will be able to feel a bit of what he is feeling.
- Active listening gives the children the opportunity to correct you. In other words, you paraphrase what the child said to you, and he tells you you're crazy (because you got it wrong). It's ok! You can fix misunderstandings.

Giving Active Listening a Chance

You can actively listen anytime and anywhere. You can say, "I want to hear what you think about <a certain subject> and I am not going to say anything until you are done. When you finish, I'll tell you what you said and what I heard." If you think this might confuse the child, try a casual approach. Simply listen silently and then paraphrase without calling attention to what you are doing: "So you are saying <repeat what you heard>. You feel <your interpretation of their feelings>. Did I get it right?" It may feel weird at first, but will get easier over time.

Things can and possibly will go wrong in active listening when you make these mistakes:

- When you hear only what you want to hear.
- When you allow your beliefs and attitudes to interfere with your listening.
- You pay attention only to how the information is being communicated (body language), not what is being spoken.
- When you are too literal. Kids have their own dialects or ways of speaking, and if you listen to the words too closely, you may get lost.
- When you listen only for the facts. How the child feels about what he is telling you may be as important. When you paraphrase back what has been said, make sure to include how you think the child is feeling. Let them correct you if you are wrong.

Communicating with Step Children

Honest communication has to be the only policy when it comes to the step family. Withdrawing in an attempt to save yourself will backfire on you. The family will continue its biological bond, and you will be left out in the cold.

Whatever you do, make sure not to lecture. I guarantee if you shake your finger at a child, he definitely will not hear what you are saying. Kids are also deaf to stories with a moral. Save your breath.

A child, whether biological or step, will tune you out if you:

- Talk to them in a wrong or cross way.
- Talk with them, not at them or to them.
- Accuse them.

Instead, try to:

- Always tell the truth.
- Make sure to use active listening.
- Try not to ever let your disagreements escalate.
- Try to keep to the specifics.

Daily Communication

Family identity is built through shared experiences. Your family identity is enhanced the more you eat meals together. Civilization was built around the dinner table. Breaking bread together, a symbolic international peace-making gesture, has more than a political meaning, it is a vital way of touching base as a family.

Mealtimes are an important part of sharing family time together, far too often dismissed in our rushed culture. Our family tries (and most times succeeds) in eating dinner together at least four nights a week, plus weekend brunches. This time is important to us. We all share what is going on in our lives.

As a step-parent, your daily communications with your step children should involve three points:

- Respectful communication – This is simple. You gain your step children's respect by showing them respect. Children learn by their role models.
- Show affection through communication - Communication is not what you say. It is also how you say it, and it involves your body language. Not all people are comfortable expressing their deepest thoughts and emotions with words. Even for those who are, words are not always enough.
- Communicate your expectations and goals

Affection does not always involve touching. You may not be a naturally touchy person. Young children have a biological need for physical affection, but physical affection does not always feel natural in a step family, nor is it always appropriate

Whether your step children are toddlers or teens or somewhere in-between it is important to have individual types of nonverbal communication with them. Talk together about how much physical affection you all feel comfortable with.

Communicate Your Expectations and Goals

Preconceived expectations of what step family life should be like are never helpful. Once the new step family has formed, however, the kids need to know what is expected in terms of family structure and need to know what behaviors are acceptable and expected of them. Kids need to understand these three points:

- Family expectations - These are moral- and value-based expectations about how people in the family should behave and treat each other.
- Personal expectations - These are achievement-based expectations children and adults have, such as goals and expectations for academic, athletic, and developmental growth.
- Relationship expectations - These are socially based expectations: "I expect you and your step sister to cooperate when you are cleaning up your room."

Setting Values

Part of defining your expectations and goals, whether personal or for the family, is about understanding your values. You have at least a vague sense of your values and how the values will fit into your image of the ideal step family life.

The first step is to sit down with the family and make a list of what values are important to everyone. The core family values are not so much a set of specifics ("Put the toilet seat down when you are done") as a set of behavior guidelines which reflect the underlying values ("We listen to everyone's opinion"). The list of core family values is sort of like a mission statement. This mission statement states explicitly how you (the family) expect family members to behave.

Here are a few questions to talk about as you begin developing your own core family values list:

- How do I want people to treat me?
- What is the best way to let one know how I feel?
- How do we feel about physical violence? Is it okay to hit someone when you are mad?
- How do I feel about my personal space?
- How do I feel about others personal space?
- How do I feel about the things I own?
- What manners are important to me?
- How do I want to be approached if there is a disagreement?

The answers to these questions will begin to form your family list. The values your write should be nonspecific enough to apply to everyone. Make sure to limit the number of values. If you keep them basic, you will do fine. Now, re-write the list and it should look similar to the following:

1. We use words to tell others how we feel. We do not name-call or use foul language.
2. We do not hurt others physically or emotionally.
3. We do not damage each other's property or our own.
4. We will not hold a grudge. We will work to solve a problem and move on.
5. We will remember to say please and thank you at all times.
6. We will respect other people's personal space.
7. When we are angry, we will not be accusatory or place blame.
8. We will think before we speak.
9. We will be responsible for our own actions.

10.   We will all take part in the household chores.

When you are done, you can post the list on the refrigerator, or a communication board, where everyone will see them on a regular basis.

Just Communicate

Although you don't want to bug your child with constant questions on how they are doing, it is important to give him frequent chances to express his feelings about the new family arrangement. If conversations are too direct, try emailing, texting, or using a shared journal to write back and forth to each other. With younger children, you can try role-playing with dolls or toys, or drawing a story together about how the child is feeling. Be on the lookout for nonverbal clues as well.

Our communication both verbal and nonverbal, are the key to a successful transition.

Financial Concerns

When deciding to commit to each other the financial discussion is usually left for last. In my opinion, it should be one of the first things you discuss. You need to know each other's financial obligations before the "I do's". Often times, most don't find out until later the other person was basically drowning in debt. Knowing what you are getting into before you take the marital step is vital. Not only does it help with communication, but also helps with trust. If you cannot trust your partner to come clean about their finances before the marriage commitment, what else might your partner try and hide from you.

Having "THE" Discussion

It is always important to ask the right questions before you get married, but if you or your future partner has children, here are a few more to add to the list:

- What are the ongoing financial responsibilities? You need to know how much alimony (ex-spousal support) or child support your future partner is receiving or paying, how long it will last, whether it can be adjusted, and what commitments are there concerning college bills. You also need to be concerned with existing credit card bills, car payments and other monthly debt payments. Ex-spousal support (alimony) often ends if the recipient remarries or lives with a partner, but child support goes on. The new partner does not have a legal obligation to support step children, so you should be clear going in about the financial realities of your own situation.

- How much do you spend on your children? You will want to consider allowances, trips, gifts and other extras. What do the children expect? What types of promises have been made in regards to special events in their life (new car at age 16 or graduation or full payment of college tuition?) Most times single parents often overspend on their children to make up for the turmoil in their life. In a blended family, you may need to walk a path between the wicked step-parent and the overindulgent fairy godparent.

- Where will you live? Do you live in his/her house or yours? Maybe neither? Starting over with a new house to meet the needs of your new family may be the best solution, although you need to be sensitive to issues such as uprooting school aged children. You also need to take into account the ex-spouse and the children. The intent is not to alienate the ex-spouse. The children need both parents. Will you share the moving costs, deposits, down payments, etc., of the move? Under present tax laws, you can each sell your home and pocket as much as $250,000 in tax-free gain as long as you have lived in and owned your residence for two of the past five years. There is no longer a requirement to trade up, so you have more flexibility in finding your new home. Most couples own the home as joint tenants with right of survivorship so the house would pass directly to the surviving spouse. However, you may consider owning the house as tenants in common, because then you can own unequal shares (if one spouse contributes the down payment, for example) and you specify your heirs in your will. Consult with an attorney or tax accountant to see what would best fit your needs.

- Will you keep one checkbook or two? Budgetary issues should be worked out ahead of time. Are you each going to contribute one-half to the family budget, or will you contribute proportionally according to your income? Either way can work. Make sure each of you has a portion of discretionary money. If you keep separate accounts, start building a joint fund for vacations, home projects, and other shared expenses.

- What will your new tax bracket be? You will both need to seek the advice of a financial planner or accountant and project your new tax bracket. Brace yourself for the marriage tax penalty. If both of you work, you will pay more as a couple than two single working people. If you or your spouse was filing as head of household, the new tax bite can be even worse. Make sure you and your ex-spouse are clear on who claims the children as dependents. This should be written in the divorce papers. I can't stress enough for you to speak with a financial planner or accountant because the tax laws change yearly.

- What are your plans on how to pay for college for your children? New partners often keep college funds separate, but it can be tough if you do not have shared philosophies and resources. If the children are of high school age, their expectations have already been set. It is easier to build a common fund and common expectations if the children are younger, but remember, even children in traditional families often choose colleges with different price tags. Fair does not mean equal. Consult with a financial planner or accountant to see what would work best financially. Consult with a college planner on what alternatives (loans, grants, 529's or scholarships) are available for college tuition.

- What type of Estate Planning will there be? Will there be a prenuptial agreement? If so, your to-do list is shorter. Otherwise, you will still both need to write new wills and check the beneficiaries on life insurance policies, retirement plans and IRAs. The presumption typically is the biological parent (your ex-spouse) would be the guardian if something happened to you. However, make sure to designate in your will a second person in the event your ex-spouse is not in your child's life. There are times when parents who remarry wish to leave their assets to their children. Others leave specific assets (such as a life insurance policy) to their children and the rest to their new spouse. By setting up a trust, you can leave your assets to your children, but allow your surviving partner to draw from it as needed during his lifetime. Consult an experienced estate-planning lawyer who has worked with blended families. You should also discuss powers of attorney, living wills and medical consent forms. Make sure all parties, including the children (if of age to understand), know your wishes.

When it comes to money, expect emotions to fly between you and your partner, between your partner and your partner's ex, and between you and your partner's ex. If you are a combined family, you may also face problems between you and your ex-partner too. All the experts suggest trying to separate financial and emotional problems between the ex-partners so each can be dealt with individually.

Handling the History

It may be difficult to deal with when you realize you don't have your partner all to yourself. The fact is your partner had a history before you and the history involved kids who now have an impact on your life. It may be difficult to understand, but because there are children involved, your partner's ex's financial matters are your financial matters, too.

It might be helpful to keep these points in mind:

- It is your partner's job to work out the money situation with the ex-partner.
- You stay out of it.
- You have no control over how money is spent in the other household. Here is a complaint so common it verges on stereotype: No matter how much child support you and your partner send, the children turn up on visiting day in clothing too small or has holes. This is a battle you will rarely win. Decide if it is worth fighting. Tolerance and an ability to remember to breathe deeply are wonderful assets for step-parents.
- Money is the great cover-up and catch-all. Other issues, namely emotional ones, hide behind money arguments.
- Money arguments can be an excuse for rehashing the old relationship and hanging onto old ties (even if the relationship has turned ugly). Do not let yourself fall into old habits.
- If your partner pays child support, the ex-partner may feel dependent. This is not a normal situation. You need to be dependent on yourself.
- It is hard but necessary at times to ignore and put up with an ex-partners' "poor me" syndrome. Be fair, make arrangements your conscience can live with, and ignore the rest.
- While few ex-partners and new partners manage to plan their finances all together, this is not possible or even desirable for most families. Do not even try it.
- Throwing money at a problem does not make it go away. You cannot buy the children's affections. Guilt and loneliness are not a reason to give children lavish and expensive gifts. It will not bring the child closer to you. Trust me, it will cause more harm than good. The step children often get in on the money act. Kids are especially skilled at blackmail by cries of "My Mommy would let me have it." Children need to learn each household has their

own monetary priorities. You can be gently assertive about this without trashing the other biological parent. Never trash the other biological parent in front of the children. This is unacceptable on all levels.

Always talk about money in a straightforward fashion. Children adjust to less money and privilege if you communicate the situation in a respectful fashion and in ways clearly understood.

Money is the root of all evil. You may agree in theory the financial affairs between your partner and their ex, are not your business, yet you may feel agitated about the time your partner spends negotiating. You may feel envious of the possessions and privileges of your partner's ex, especially if you are struggling to help support your step children. You may even feel envious of the presents your partner buys for your step child. But, do not fall into the jealousy trap. Would you want to walk a mile in their shoes? I doubt it.

Introductions

Preparing to Meet the Children

Whether it is early or later in the relationship, the first meeting is an important event. Advance planning is the key. A successful experience is an experience where everyone walks away feeling more comfortable, not less comfortable. Ideally you want the first meeting to be casual and avoid pitfalls.

Before the first meeting, follow these tips:

- Define your expectations for the meeting, and lower your goals. It is not going to be love-at-first-sight, and it should not be. Think of it in biological terms. You are encroaching on another persons' territory. Be polite and wary. This meeting is not about love or fun. It is about getting through it alive so you can live to see meeting #2.
- Think of meeting the kids for the first time as a blind date. What are the secrets to a successful blind date? According to my single pals, it is simple: Keep it short and safe. Try an activity everyone will like, such as a park or a movie. Do not be over-ambitious: A full day at Disney World will leave the kids (and you already-stressed-out adults) tired, wired, and wasted. Keep it to a couple of hours at most. A meal may not be a great idea, because you will be facing each other across a table for a long while, and this may be too much for the kids to handle right away.

- Relax. (Easy for me to say, I know.) Consciously accept this may be stressful, and take five minutes to let your tensions go. Breathe!

Introducing Your New Friend to Your Children

It takes time to get to know a person before you jump into another marriage or serious relationship. You have to keep in mind when children are involved things are not so easy. If you are thinking about settling down with someone who argues with you and has no patience with children, you are going to have a tough time maneuvering through the normal issues of raising a well-blended family. If you know you are in love and do not mind constant conflict, this could be a choice for you. I know, through experience, being in a nurturing environment has made it a million times easier to have a great life.

When you feel you have made the decision and are ready to move on to the next step, there are several things you can do.

Here are a few ways to introduce your new partner to your children:

- Invite your partner for dinner at your home but make sure he brings your children gifts of relatively forbidden items (like candy).
- Plan to have dinner together at a kid-friendly restaurant, and definitely let them have dessert at his request.
- Have your new partner come over for an evening to watch cartoons or play video games.
- Take a trip to the zoo or other favorite kid hangout.

Let your children get to know your new partner in small doses and wait for them to ask about them on their own. Patience now can be a great asset later.

Taking it Slow

Once you have introduced your new friend to your children you do not want to immediately set up household. You should not have overnight visits until the children become comfortable with the idea that your friend is here to stay. You can certainly choose whatever is comfortable for you, but if you take this slowly you lower the risk of emotional backlash from your children while adjusting to your new life. Keep in mind the children may feel threatened, fearful they could lose you to this new person or the new person will change the rules of the family.

Here are several things to warn your partner about when first meeting your children:

- Avoid trying to show immediate signs of affection. Even an enthusiastic high five can be greeted by a suspicious icy stare.
- Do not call a child over the age of two by any condescending names. If you call a child a baby you might expect to set back your cause by several points.
- Never discipline the child in a harsh manner, particularly if it appears to contradict the methods used in the household.
- Do not argue about anything with the biological parent in front of the children. A child is leery of new people and will see even minor bickering as a threat. When trust has been established you are free to go at it as any normal couple would do.
- Do not be overly affectionate when the children are around. The children may still have fantasies of their biological parents

getting back together. Too much in-their-face smooching will make them feel edged out of the relationship. The child will react by acting out to gain more attention.

Different Reactions

Each child adjusts to a new relationship in his own way. It is best to give the new relationships time to grow at a pace which works for each person involved. You cannot force harmony. At first, when you begin a new relationship involving your children and a new person in your life, expect everyone to be at odds. You are likely to be excited about starting a new life while your children will be desperately trying to cling to the old. It will be crazy for a while, but with patience, understanding, and love, it can work out.

Prepping Your Kids to Meet Your Partner's Kids

Before the kids—your kids and your new love's kids—meet each other, you will need to prepare. Do not throw them all in a room together and expect it to work. It might, but then again it might not, and this is too important to leave to random chance.

Here are steps to take to make sure the meeting goes as smooth as it possibly can:

- Do not be discouraged if your child instantly hates your new partner's children. Give it time, talk with both of them (alone), make sure misunderstandings are cleared up, and then stand back. Let them work it out.
- Assess each child's temperament and needs as honestly as you can.

- Talk to the kids about the meeting, but keep it cool. Let them know ahead of time they are about to meet other kids who may, someday, be their new siblings.
- If you have teens or preteens meeting other teens or preteens, be aware of possible sexual energy and tension.
- Plan an activity. Everyone staring at each other in a living room or restaurant may not be fun.
- If you are combining young kids and older kids, gear the activity toward the youngest common denominator, or toward the child who has the most needs. A tantrum or meltdown will prevent anything else from working.
- The meeting place or activity should take place where there are opportunities for kids to retreat.
- Keep the activity to the length of a birthday party. This means no weekends away, at least until you all know each other better.

Introducing the Kids to Others

Now how are you going to introduce them? If you do not think about it ahead of time, it can get awkward. Much depends on how everyone is feeling about the relationship. Much also depends on the child's age. Teenagers are notoriously embarrassed by their parents, whether biological or step-parent. Now is the time to rise above the petty stresses and be the kids' ally by being conscious and sensitive to their sensitivities.

Introduce the children first. When introducing the kids to others you might say - this is "my boyfriend's children" or "my partner's children." This term, when spoken in a detached manner, relinquishes all responsibility. The kids will not feel threatened by you, but also may not believe you care. If spoken with warmth when the relationship between you and the kids is on an even keel, it merely describes the configuration.

Once the kids are comfortable with each other, remember siblings fight. It is normal. Don't try and get between the kids. Allow them to work out their differences in an acceptable manner.

Do Not Leap to Conclusions

No matter how good or how poorly the first few encounters go, it is important to remember while first impressions and first reactions are important, these impressions are not necessarily true indicators of how all your relationships will change, grow, and develop over time. What you think and feel now is not necessarily what you all are going to think and feel later.

Relationships are a process. First meetings are important: First meetings can help smooth the way, but are not the only determining factors in the relationship. As you will learn, things will both ease up and get harder. Try to look at the big picture.

Winning Over Your Partner's Child

As you think about your role as a step-parent, remember to turn the tables, and consider your own kids' needs and your partner's relationship with them.

- Do not ignore the child. No one likes to be ignored, and ignoring children does not work anyway. The child will get more insistent and louder.
- Do not judge them.

- Consider the child's feelings, wishes, and plans. Have the parent ask permission to invite a friend (you) over for dinner. It is the children's house too, you know, and you are asking to spend time with their parent.

- Hold back. Let the child come to you. There is lots of time for intimacy.

- Realize a bad reaction may not be to you. The child may need assuring he will be loved and cared for as he was before the divorce. Go slow.

- Remember dating relationships can provide good role models. You are not evil for being there. If you believe it, you are on the road to having the kid believe it, too.

- Concentrate on your love relationship, not your relationship with the whole family. The love and respect you are building forms the foundation of your relationship and, if you choose to take it further, of the family.

- Wait for the kids to realize they cannot and will not scare you away. You are not trying to replace their parent, you are not trying to steal their parent, and you are respectful of them. Over time and with the right treatment, the kids will see the joy and happiness you bring to their parent.

- And in case the adult love of your life is not reading this book, too, and you have young children at home, make sure you share the above words of wisdom with them. You want your children's hearts to be won over too, right?

Jealousy

The kids are expressing jealousy—is there a special reason? Are the children being cut out of the loop? Is there too much hand-holding and smooching going on? Children are often jealous of their parent's friends, dates, and lovers. It is important for them to see their parent has friends.

If a child is expressing jealousy, take a walk in his shoes. He has been through changes, so be patient. Do not scold the child. Sit and talk with them. Be an active listener. Suggest a small, shared outing. Keep it short and make yourself a bit scarce for a while so the biological parent and child can enjoy their reunion.

There are times when meeting away from the children is the best dating solution, especially in the beginning and during stressful times. It is easier on kids, easier on you, and easier on the parent, who does not have to deal with jealousy or resentment from either side.

Never apologize for having a new friend. If things get too tense or stressful, suggest counseling. We talk about counseling in another chapter.

Family Rules and Discipline

First Things First

What's the difference between core family values, family rules, and limits? We have already learned core family values are a general set of behavior guidelines applying to everyone in the family: "We solve our problems with words." Family rules are more specific: "Homework must be finished before game time is allowed." Limits are specific behavior boundaries for each child. "Aaron cannot cross the street without a grown-up."

When deciding on your family's approach to discipline, ask yourselves this question: "How do we want this family to function, and what actions should we take when things break down?" Rules and limits are more specific than values. Rules are how the core family values, which are general, are expressed. In a family, but especially in a step family, kids need to understand specifically what is expected of them (the rules), and they need to understand their boundaries (the limits).

Evidence from numerous studies has shown positive reinforcement, when used consistently, is more effective in changing behavior than negative enforcement or punishment. Positive reinforcement has been shown to strengthen behavior through praise and rewards. Negative reinforcement refers to the application of a negative action such as taking things away or physical punishment. Knowing what limits to set can be tricky. The limits should be modified as the child grows. Whatever manner you choose, make sure to be consistent and make sure if applies to all children involved.

A disciplinary approach and action work best when it comes from joint decisions made by you and your partner. If you are not consistent, the kids are going to play you off, one against the other. Children also need the security of seeing the two of you as a solid unit. The couple, as the keystone of the step family, should provide a unified front, even if you are still struggling with each other about family matters. When two families combine, providing consistency and a unified front become even more challenging.

Sit down together with your partner and go over the list. You may need to talk about it in several sessions. As you work on developing your family rules, write down what you come up with.

Here are questions to use as a guide:

- What will the responsibilities be for household chores?
- What specific activities are not allowed in our house?
- Who takes responsibility for pets?
- Are there food or mealtime rituals important to us?
- What is an agreed upon curfew?
- What are the homework rules?
- At what age is makeup appropriate?
- Are there limits on use of the TV, computer, car, phone or video games?
- Will there be dating rules? Age?
- What are our feelings on our teenagers being sexually active? Using drugs? Drinking alcohol or smoking? Piercings?
- What are our religious beliefs and how much participation do we expect our children to have in them?
- How will we ensure our privacy is respected?

- What is our policy on guests? Should the kids ask first before inviting their friends over to the house?

You have determined an approach to discipline and made a few decisions, the main question comes up again: What about discipline and the step-parent? What part is done by you and what part does the biological parent handle?

At first, the direct assigning of limits and consequences should be left up to the biological parent, and you should avoid taking a direct role. This way you are not immediately sabotaging the relationship you are trying to build. Be patient. The process for kids to begin to accept discipline from a step-parent is about two years. It takes about two years to grow a strong and trusting relationship.

When you do start to move into a role of discipline, take it slow, do not charge full ahead. You may ruin the relationship you took so long to build. Remember discipline is the entire process of raising a child. You can and should be a good role model, treat the kids with respect, and encourage and reward them for appropriate behavior.

You will need to bite your tongue at times. You can drag your partner into another room to discuss discipline, but your partner has to be the decision maker and the enforcer.

Yes, leave matters of discipline to the biological parent for a while, but do not be a pushover when it comes to your own rights. You are a member of the household. You need privacy and consideration. It is also important your step children understand you and their parent are a disciplinary team. As time goes on, children need to begin to see you, too, as an authority figure. If you feel your rights or feelings are being stomped on, you may have to step in and assert yourself. Be prepared for conflict. Your partner should be your ally here.

As you move into more of an authority role, you can begin to enforce already established rules and regulations. Continue to take a backseat role by using reminders of what was established as the family rules. Remember it may take a while and be hard work for the biological parent to feel comfortable with you making disciplinary choices for her child.

Once the entire family is comfortable with one another, then you can move more into the role of the one who can discipline. Once you have lived together for a while and are comfortable with everyone, then you can begin to make independent decisions about discipline without deferring to your partner. It is appropriate to make spontaneous disciplinary choices in these instances:

- When the biological parent is not available
- When there are no established consequences for the misbehavior

Children are exceptional at maintaining their position in their homes. To them it is a matter of emotional survival. You would not believe how much a child, even one of average intelligence, can manipulate a situation in order to maintain a sense of security. If you cause the child to feel threatened, do not be surprised to find subtle efforts of sabotage.

Manipulation is not necessarily evil and mean-spirited. Children may not be conscious of why they are doing something. The children are only looking at the immediate result they want to achieve. If the child is worried daddy loves the new wife more and will abandon him, he will look for ways to survive—maybe by developing an illness with real symptoms. Maybe, through naughty behavior, the child will find ways to pit one parent against the other. A child can be aware of what will upset everyone and will not hesitate to use this primitive form of intuition.

Resentment often boils out into those hurtful words of "You are not my <mom or dad> you cannot tell me what to do." These words hurt and are meant to. Respond with calm authority in your voice. Here are three not-so-harsh comebacks to help you:

- I live here and this is my house. You need to listen to me.
- I am not your parent, but I am the adult in charge right now. I am reminding you of the rules.
- I am your step-parent, and you do need to listen to me.

Children need discipline in their lives to know what is expected of them. Children must have structure to make them feel secure, loved and a valuable part of the family. These rules can apply in all types of situations:

- Explain the rules in an age appropriate way for each child.
- Be consistent. This is the most important item. Make sure to be consistent with every child.
- Lower your voice, which will force them to listen.
- Let the punishment fit the wrong doing.
- Do not name call.
- Once the punishment is over – let it go. Do not hold a grudge over it. Stay in the present.

Two Houses, Two Sets of Rules

When you have shared custody of the children, it is common for issues to come up about the differences in the rules of each household. Take a back seat here, too. It is your partner's job to deal with his ex-partner. Your partner and his/her ex-partner should communicate about such matters, and then your partner can share the information with you. Unless it is unavoidable, do not rely only on the child's report.

You may fear the kids will be confused by having two households and two sets of rules. Kids are smart and adapt faster than you think. Remember you and your partner have no control over what goes on at the ex-partners house. Make sure the child explicitly understands the values and rules in your household, and the role modeling you are providing will make an impression on them. If you feel, however, there is physical, sexual, or emotional abuse going on in the other household, do not let it slide. Get help immediately. Better safe than sorry.

Whatever discipline approach you choose, make sure the children know you are both in agreement and will support each other's decisions.

You Need Privacy

Keeping the Spark

Effective parent-stepparent teams begin with healthy marriages. Your marriage will be affected by the lack of privacy. This is part of having kids in the house. Not only are the children there physically, also emotionally. Communication plays a key part in keeping the spark.

If you are the custodial parent, or share custody, or have the children often, you might feel like your sex life has been impeded. Yes, romantic life with a parent is unlike the single life. You cannot chase each other naked through the house, you are going to have to be quiet, and you run the risk of being interrupted.

The first year or so is the hardest on your sex life, when the honeymoon hormones are flying at the same time you are doing all of this adjusting. It will be important to establish a couple of house rules:

- Everyone must knock on closed bedroom doors before entering and must wait for an answer.
- Assert your need for private time.
- Respect their personal space and the children will be more apt to return the favor.

Private time is not just about sex—you also need intimacy. During a stressful visit or hard time in family life, you have to be able to check in with each other. Sometimes this means making love, and other times this means lying on the bed playing cards, talking, or giving each other massages.

It is vital to talk with each other, even if it is about almost nothing. The craziness of the world we live in, combined with the craziness of children, can kill conversational opportunities. Do not let it. Talking is an essential part of intimacy.

One way to get privacy is to leave together, without the kids. Hiring a baby-sitter has its problems. The kids are too young or too old, and sitters are expensive. But dating is important. Set up a date night at least once a week. Watch your friend's children and they watch yours. This way you both get time without the children. You must have time alone as a couple.

It is no secret children who observe loving relationships with physical affection grow up to become loving, affectionate adults.

Take time to nurture your relationship, date on a regular basis, learn to communicate and resolve conflict, and enjoy a healthy sexual relationship. Make your marriage a priority.

Surprise Custody

It can happen. You marry your new partner, aware there are children in the picture, but way in the distance. Though you know your partner has kids, you have downplayed their importance since the children are not going to live with you. Maybe the kids live far away, and maybe there are regular visits. But essentially, your house is your own. Then, surprise, for whatever reason (death in the family, junior not doing good in school, the biological parent flips out, or moves and the child wants to stay in the neighborhood), now the child or children are moving in. I know you are feeling panicked, and guilty for feeling panicked.

Your biggest struggle may be the fight to remain quiet. The child may be upset, and you will not help move things into a positive direction if he overhears you yelling at your spouse in the bedroom about how you do not want to be living with their child. That said – this should be been cleared up before moving forward with the relationship if you were not willing to live full time with the children.

Surprise custody often happens during the teenage years when the cute little boy now towers and booms over his mother, or the little girl is busting out of her bra—and her room at night. The overwhelmed parent, throwing up her hands, sends the overgrown child to live with the other biological parent. The rebellious child, who may have been romanticizing about the idea of life with the noncustodial parent, is often all too ready to go.

Kids are smart. They can pick up on when they are not wanted. If this is the case, talk with the child. Assure him though this is a circumstance no one asked for, you are a family and families stick together. Problems get solved by talking about them and working on them. You are all in this together.

The biological parent should play a large role in the adjustment, reassuring them they are wanted and welcomed, and being actively involved in their life. No turning back.

Be aware you are in an adjustment period, and it may take you and the child a bit of time. As the emergency step-parent, take care to nurture yourself. You need to relax, take lots of walks and call all of your friends and family for support.

Complaint Mode

It is easy to complain about things going wrong whether it is about your natural family or your step family. If complaining helps you to validate your feelings, then by all means complain. Make sure to discuss with your partner what you are feeling. Resolve the feelings and the issues and move on.

Top Biological Parent Complaints:

1. My partner is too harsh on my kids. Kids are not perfect—they are kids!
2. My partner knew I had kids before we were married. Why does he think the expectations on our time together should change?
3. My partner wants to take over. I did fine when I was by myself.
4. My partner is so jealous when I talk with my ex-partner. I have to. We have to be able to work together for the kid's sake. He does not understand how hard these meetings are.
5. My partner wants the kids to love her like their own parent. Children should not be pushed so hard.
6. Just because you miss your own kids, you should not be angry with or ignore mine.
7. I want to have more children, but my partner doesn't.
8. My partner talks down to my children – not to them. He does not listen to them.
9. The kids come over, and my partner withdraws.

10.   I feel stuck in the middle between her and the kids. I am always playing mediator, making sure all sides are okay.

11.   My partner gets jealous of the kids, the attention I pay them, and what I buy them.

12.   I do not get enough support. It is all so hard, and my partner and my kids should be more supportive of me.

Top Step-parent Complaints

1.   No one appreciates or respects me for how much work I do for everyone. I feel like a third wheel.

2.   All our decisions about money and vacations have to be cleared with the ex-partner. I want to be head of my own household.

3.   When the kids are here, I feel neglected. When the kids are away, I have to comfort her because the kids are missed. When do we get to be a couple? Where is the romance?

4.   There is no privacy around here.

5.   I want a baby, and my partner does not.

6.   We fight about money. We are on a budget. I should not be left to feel I am in the wrong by trying to keep our budget. He is so scared his kids will leave him he will not discipline them, and he buys them anything they want.

7.   My kids are the ordinary, everyday kids, but when my partner's kids arrive, they are treated special and my kids are ignored.

8.   My partner expects me to take over and be the parent, to make everything better. Last I knew we were supposed to share responsibility.

9.   His ex-partner is a too much a part of our lives. I know the children are his kids too, they communicate far too much. I

do not want his negative energy in my household. It is our household and things are not the same as before.

If you marry a person much older or younger than yourself you may encounter most of these issues and more. If you marry someone who has never had children and you have children there may be other issues to deal with, however the issues above are the majority and these issues are certainly not the end of the world. One last thing, depending on who makes the most money in the relationship you will encounter the issue of the partner making the most money wanting to help their children out financially. Make sure to discuss what you plan to do and/or spend with your partner. Do not do things behind their back. It will come back to haunt you.

New Baby

Once you have decided to have a new baby, or you are already pregnant, or the adoption papers have been filed, now what? How are you going to tell the kids? And how are your kids and step kids going to react? How will you tell your ex-partner? Or better yet, how will you tell the grandparents?

How to Tell the Children

If the kids are old enough to understand, have the biological parent raise the subject of a new baby before the pregnancy, to get them accustomed to the idea. Once again, this should be done by the biological parent. Also, if you tell the kids you are thinking about having a baby, be prepared for them to tell their other biological parent. Do not be surprised if the children reject the idea. Let them voice their objections. Listen to their objections. Let it go and then when the pregnancy occurs, tell them your happy news and most likely the kids will be accepting because they will have had time to process the idea.

How to Tell the Ex-Partner

Chances are if you have told the children, they have already told the ex-partner. Do not leave this one to the kids. You need to be the one to tell them. Your partner should tell his ex-partner, and you should tell yours. It does not matter you are not lovers or even friends anymore. What affects a child also affects a parent. Consider it a courtesy call to someone you have a working relationship with, and consider it will affect them emotionally.

A relationship breaking up is one thing, and a remarriage is another, but having a child with another person makes it final the former relationship is over. The ex-partner does not need to be the first person on the list. Waiting until the pregnancy is viable (after the first trimester) or the adoption papers are in order is always wise.

How to Tell the Grandparents

Because you are no longer married to your ex-partner does not mean your children are not connected to their grandparents. The grandparents need to be supportive of their grandchildren and their new sibling. Discuss with your ex-partner whether or not they want to be the one to contact their parents or if you should. Again, waiting until the pregnancy is viable (after the first trimester) or the adoption papers are in order is best.

During the Pregnancy

Jealousy and anxiety are common before the baby arrives. Kids may fear being replaced. Young children often do not seem to react much to such an announcement. It is too vague, and the child is too young to understand. The child may as time goes on, enjoy feeling the baby move in their mother or stepmother's belly.

Kids of all ages tend to get excited and anxious though they may not immediately show it. Incorporate them into the planning. Solicit their input on names, and help them feel part of the process.

After Baby Arrives

It's a baby! It's our baby! For step families with children from one or both partners, the new baby brings something in common to everyone, and a sense of permanence and completion to the family. If you were not truly combined before, you are now.

Life in the step family with a new baby is no doubt more hectic than before, and it will be happier. Babies are delightful.

The children's reaction to the infant is not always warm and welcoming. The eldest child may feel her family position is threatened, as here comes along a new eldest for the blended family. The youngest child may mourn his lost position as "family baby" as he moves to a "middle child" position. Younger children may revert back to baby tendencies. Be patient and firm. Reassure the children nothing will change in the way you love and care for them. If handled incorrectly, and if the parents are too wrapped up in their new baby to reassure the older children, a new baby can block the relationship between kid, biological parent, and step-parent.

Fortunately, the results can be more positive. Once the baby is born, the children generally relate to their new half-sibling the way kids always relate to siblings. Half-siblings are brothers and sisters to each other. The kids will build their own relationships, and will have their own pleasures and disappointments with each other. You do not have control over their relationship.

Teenager Reactions

For a teenager between the ages of 13 and 17, the idea of having a pregnant mother or stepmother is about enough to make him curl up and die with embarrassment. Your step child does not want to know you are having sex. The idea is repulsive, horrifying, humiliating and gross.

Unfortunately for your sensitive step child, remarriages are often more sexually charged than first marriages, especially at first. And sex is harder to ignore.

Here are a few specific hints for teens:

- Look for the positive intent.
- Do not automatically limit your step child's involvement.
- Encourage them to be involved in their baby half-brother or half-sister's life, but do not assume the teen will automatically babysit.

Different Surnames

Legally, you can give your new child any last name you want, but if you and your partner, or you and your kids, have other surnames, you will have to decide which one to use. (You can make up your own, too.) Depending upon whether or not you took your new partners last name, you can hyphen names to include both last names.

Parenting is Not Like Step-parenting

If you have step-parented but not parented, you will be surprised at the depth of your emotional attachment to the new baby. Be prepared for surprises. New parents find themselves changing their minds on parenting issues. The disapproving step-parent who felt their partner was far too lenient on disciplinary issues now lightens up, loosens up, and realizes kids are not perfect. Step-parents often become better step-parents once they are parents.

Step-parents tend to make wonderful biological parents. They have already had experience with kids, and are already committed to family life.

Step-parents also commonly start to feel closer to their step children after they have had a child of their own. This is because they are more focused in on children. Often a step-parent will fall in love with her step children when she sees how much the children love and feel close to the baby.

A new baby usually has a positive effect on the partnership. You and your partner now share something so vital in common you have more of an equal partnership. For the step-parent who has never parented before, gaining official parenthood status can help diminish old power struggles. This renewed enthusiasm often plays out as more attention paid to the older kids. It is a definitely a win-win situation.

When Step Children Visit

Visiting step children often have the most resistance to the step family. The children want to spend time with the biological parent they rarely get to see, but because you are like a stranger, they do not feel particularly close to you. Visiting step children often feel excluded from the family identity. Be sympathetic. Shared experiences have occurred without them, so the children have reasons for feeling left out.

You can help make a child feel more a part of the family by following these pointers:

- Creating a place for each child, even if it is a shelf, a closet, a bed, a dresser drawer, or a corner. Do not touch their stuff.
- Give the child public acknowledgment (but keep it subtle so as not to embarrass them). Adding the child's name to the mailbox: John, Jane, and Joseph Smith will help.
- Introduce your step children to what you do in your daily life, whether it is a special group meeting, a club, or other type of event.
- Try to spend time with each child alone.

The First Time

The first time the step children come over for a sleepover visit (long or short) is a pivotal moment in the step family's history. As a step-parent, you may feel desperate to make them happy and to make sure you are accepted. You may also want to casually greet them and go on with life, letting the kids fit in as they can. Both emotions may exist.

Once the children arrive, you may find yourself again conflicted. They may not be what you expected at all, even if you have spent casual time with them before. The children may have been accepting, friendly, enthusiastic, and affectionate. Now you may find the sweet young children are no longer sweet. They may be simply unlike the kids you thought you knew, simply because kids change quickly as a natural part of growth and maturing. Or you may find you like them, but they take more time and energy—energy you were not expecting to spend.

This first visit has your partner flipped out too—either worried sick the child will not accept the new arrangement or acting a bit strange or changed, not as the lover you know. The tension the two of you feel may start to show in your relationship.

For the first visit, remember these pointers:

- Recognize visits may be difficult at first, and go with it.
- Take care of yourself. If you begin to feel emotionally overextended, take yourself out of the situation for a while. Take a walk, read a book, or take a nap.
- Check in with your partner on a regular basis to show you are being supportive.
- Remain open for fun. Moments of supreme pleasure often follow moments of disaster, and vice versa.

Regular Visits

When visits occur on a regular basis, things will get both easier and harder. It is a relief to settle into a schedule and to begin building a regular relationship with the children. You can get a wonderful sense of family two days a week or even two days a month. Having the kids every weekend can also be a hardship for the couple who is busy working all week. There is no time for the two of them.

Be aware of the following trouble spots:

- Do not beg to gain a step child's acceptance; it will not work.
- Be friendly and welcoming, but do not overdo it. The more you act like yourself, the sooner the child is likely to accept you.

Step-parent Visit Overload

During a visit, you might find yourself on overload. Overloaded people do strange things, depending on their coping abilities. Some people withdraw or get strange—their partner may look at them as if to say, "Who are you? Where is the person I love and married?" You may find yourself unable to relax or, worse yet, find you are acting distant. When your step child is unable to relax or is distant (which is common), the biological parent (who wants you two to love each other and get along) may panic.

The biological parent needs to stop forcing the two of you on each other. You need to lower your expectations and goals for the visit.

The Abandoned Step-parent

It is not only the step-parent and the children who start acting odd during visits. Your partner, the biological parent, is either happy or worried the kids are there and then abandon you. Where is the intimacy? Where is the way he looks at you across the table with the combination of desire and affection?

Your partner might also start acting strange, talking in another tone of voice, or snapping back into old behavior patterns. You may find yourself feeling abandoned and lonely, thinking, "I want my partner back."

Here are a few tips for the overloaded or abandoned step-parent:

- I know you are tired and feel like an outcast, but include yourself in at least a part of the activities your partner is doing with the kids. Otherwise you will begin feeling even more left out.
- Try to spend special time with each child, even if it is on an occasional basis.
- Unless your time with the children is short (in which case you do not need a break), take a break for the two of you. You need your intimacy.

Occasional Visits

If you see your step children only once or twice a year, the transition periods can be difficult for everyone. Plan a limited number of activities, and expect nothing. Remember even several weeks can be a long time for a child, especially a young one. Kids can change drastically in a short period of time, so it can be like getting a whole new set of children at each visit.

Once the children arrive, give them time to adjust before plunging wildly into activities. Welcome them into the house as a member of the family, but make sure each child gets a refresher course on the way the household is run. Remind them of the core family values and rules, and maybe discuss what the children remember from the previous visit.

When you and your partner do not see a child for months at a time, there may be a tendency to treat them like a guest and stay on your best behavior. Do not do this! It will work better for all concerned if you get real. Remember you are not putting on a show here—this is family, and part of being a family is teaching family members how to be real with each other.

On the other hand, do not be too "matter of fact". Make sure you greet and treat the child like you are happy to see him. He needs the reassurance.

As you get to know the child, try to avoid playing "Quiz the Kid": "What are you into now?" "Do you have lots of friends?" It is better to ask no questions for a while. For kids, questions are not conversation—it is interrogation. Being real does not mean being rude. Courtesy and respect are an important part of healthy family dynamics.

Do Not Try to Change Them

Your step child may arrive for the annual visit with language, manners, and clothing you do not approve of. Though you may not like this evidence of the "other" house, or you may not appreciate these new behaviors the child may be trying out on you, do not try too hard to change things. Rudeness is not acceptable, and neither is repulsive, gross behavior. When you cannot stand it anymore, you can speak out by making a general assertion of the rules: "At our house we do not wear our pants that way." But weigh effort and possible resentment against the possibility of having a decent visit, and move toward acceptance, enthusiasm, and encouragement.

You do not need to take on a parental role, but you do need to be an adult and a role model. Modeling appropriate behavior is an important part of being an effective step-parent, which means setting limits on what type of behavior you will accept around you even if the visit is short. Also, try to be sympathetic to your partner, the biological parent, who may feel sad and frustrated at this visible evidence of this lack of control, influence, and input into the child's life.

It can be tortuous to witness a visiting child exhibiting self-destructive behavior, such as smoking cigarettes, and to know you have no control over their behavior. Remember no parent, biological or step has control. You do have influence, though. Do not underestimate the power of role modeling, and let go of what you cannot change.

The Child is not a Messenger

Kids who have two households, or who live in one household but visit another parent, are often confused with loyalty issues. Do not ever use the child as a message bearer: "Tell your father if he does not pay the check on time this month, I am seeing my lawyer again!" This will backfire on you.

Do Not Try to Buy Them

When kids are only occasional members of a household, there is a tendency toward overindulgence. There is nothing wrong with a little indulgence, if it does not come at the expense of the other kids in the house, and if it is not done with ulterior motives, such as getting back at the ex-spouse or trying to buy love from the child. When parents do not see kids except on vacation, the parents want to show them how glad they are to see them. Children should be treated with respect, courtesy, responsibility, accountability, and a bit of pampering.

Semi-Combined Visits

When your children live with you all or most of the time and the other kids come to visit, things can get even more complicated. The visiting kids often feel like intruders, and may express great jealousy when they see the kids who are there all the time interacting with their biological parent. The children who live in the home may feel displaced both physically and emotionally, especially if they have to clear a space for their step siblings to sleep.

Semi-combined visits require a great deal of understanding on the part of the adults. It is not an easy situation, but it can get better over time as the kids form more of a bond.

Beginnings and Endings

Transition times (arriving and leaving) can be hard. A number of children get quiet and withdrawn. Others act out. Transitional times can be as hard on the step-parent as the child. Come to think of it, it's not so easy for the biological parent, either. The child, who is changing houses, whether it is twice a week or once a year, has to cope with new rhythms, rules, and patterns.

To help smooth the way, consider these tips:

- Allow time for everyone to detox. Expect the worst, and maybe you will be pleasantly surprised.

- Make yourself scarce for a while so you can calm down and work on your own tension levels. This also gives the child and the biological parent an opportunity to spend time alone.
- Establish rituals to help re-orient the child in your home.

Visitation Schedules

When planning the visits, whether in the courtroom or over the phone, it can be extremely stressful for everyone involved. Though the best results happen when there is flexibility, this is not always possible. Unless it is utterly unavoidable, the biological parent should never cancel on a child. The child needs the security and reassurance of knowing he is always welcome and wanted.

Visitation plans should incorporate the step-parent. Often the step-parent feels left out of the loop as the parent and the ex-spouse continue an intimate or often hostile relationship, planning times and setting up dates. Work with your partner so you do not feel forced into uncomfortable situations especially if relations are not cordial, such as waiting in the car outside the ex-spouse's house while the parent picks up the kids, or being the one to drop off the child.

Reassuring Your Own Kids

With step siblings visiting, your own children's reactions and ups and downs will certainly affect the whole family. If your children are relatively happy and secure, it will make things easier for you. It may also make it easier on the visiting kids—as they will not face hostility from your kids. The rules apply whether your kids live with you all the time, part-time, or visit.

Here are a few suggestions:

- Keep a special place private no matter how crowded conditions get when the entire family is assembled.
- Help your child anticipate what the visit will be like by talking about it ahead of time.
- Let your child know nothing has changed emotionally between you—the new kids are not crowding your affections.
- Sit down with your child and brainstorm ways to make the visiting kids welcome. By including your child in these welcoming activities, she'll feel a part of the events.
- Allow for grumpiness and plan to give her space and time to be alone—and to be alone with you.

When a Child Refuses to Visit

There are times when a child might refuse to visit your home. Your partner, the biological parent, will feel hurt, but you, too, will feel rejected and hurt.

When a child refuses to visit, try to determine why.

Here are a few possibilities:

- You might have hurt their feelings, or an old conflict was not resolved.
- The child might feel intimidated or teased by other kids in the house.
- The child might feel you cramp their lifestyle. Things like he is not allowed to have friends over, listen to his music, or dress as he prefers.

- The child may be feeling pressure from their custodial parent to shun you.
- The child may be frightened to leave their custodial parent alone because she or he is sick, or in an emotional state.
- He might feel they cannot leave the custodial parent because they need to be a protector in a violent household.

Even if your partner has visitation rights, you may not want to force a child to come visit. Encourage your partner to try to find out what's going on, offer an ear, and tell him you are ready to talk about it whenever he is. Both you and the biological parent should continue to encourage him to come and visit. When he does show up, do not say a word, and do not hold it against him.

Post-Visit

When the visit is over, you and your partner may keep the postmortem going for days. You may have no idea of how successful the visit was. Your perceptions may be different from those of your partner on this matter, too. I'll bet you feel utterly drained. Visits are exhausting. Hang in there – it does get better. Communicate with each other to validate how the visit went. Discuss making any changes for future visits.

Problem Children

A step child with problems creates problems for the entire family. High-stress behavior never happens in a vacuum. Even one member of the family losing their cool is one too many, and this affects the step family as a whole.

Divorce, separation, death, remarriage, a new family configuration—these are all hard things for a child to adjust to. Children of divorce are at risk for depression and stress, and this can sometimes turn into self-destruction, violent behavior, failing in school, and addiction. Most will show signs of stress, so don't immediately leap to thinking your step child (or your child) is doing drugs.

How will you and your partner know if the adjustment is happening? If you are new in your step child's life or not emotionally close, watching for changes in behavior may be difficult for you. You do not know the child. Here is where your partner will need to take a leadership role.

How can you and your partner tell if a kid is in trouble? There are several key signs to watch for, including these:

- School problems
- Peer relationships
- Problems at home

School Problems

Your step child's response to school is an excellent indicator of how things are going. Watch for a sudden drop in grades, change in interest, or increased absenteeism. It may be something is happening at school, or it may be a reaction to stuff going on at home. Either way, you and your partner will need to deal with it.

Peer Relationships

If you do not live with the child, it is going to be especially tough to figure out how the peer relationships are going.

Check for a change in friends. As much as you do not like to talk to your ex-spouse, you both need to keep the communication lines open to compare notes. Is your partner's straight-A-student getting piercings and hanging with the rough crowd? If the child is losing his old friends, acting belligerent, and messing up on grades, it is time to check it out. How old is he? Might it be the rebellious side of adolescence? Or perhaps you are all living in a new community and he is having trouble making new friends. Has he always been shy?

Let him know you are there for him if he needs to talk about anything going on. He may reject you, but deep down he may also feel a comfort knowing you care enough to ask.

Problems at Home

You will get your best sense of how a step child is adjusting (or not adjusting) by how she acts at home. Yes, expect quietness, especially toward you. But if you are seeing evidence of self-abuse or addiction, if the child is committing crimes, or if things are unbearably strained, your step child—and the family as a whole—may need additional help.

First Step is to Recognize

It is hard to admit your step child is in real trouble—it is human to try to deny it. But it is better to look at it now than suffer the consequences of letting it go too far.

School involvement (for you, your partner, or both) is a way to keep an eye on your step child's well-being. If the teachers know you as a concerned parent, she will be more likely to keep an eye on your child to see how he is doing. Call for a general chat. Do not wait for conference time or to be called into the office.

Self-Abuse, Eating Disorders, and Addiction

Watch out for signs of serious trouble, depression, or self-abusive behavior, especially in the teen years. Keep paying attention to what is going on, even if the child initially ignores you—the more trouble she is in, the more she will ignore you. Part of step-parenting (all parenting) means persistently showing you care, your concern, and positive reinforcement, even as the child cuts you cold. Believe me, she will hear the care in your voice, and it matters. Giving a child a sense of her own strengths will help her learn to respect her body, respect and care for herself, and feel confident enough to resist peer pressures.

Here is a list of things to look for as you assess whether your step child can use outside counseling:

- Self-abuse includes cutting, burning, extreme risk-taking, and other self-destructive behaviors. While piercings, tattoos, and branding may be the style, there is a difference between minor risk-taking and keeping up with the crowd, and major self-damage caused by depression.

- Eating disorders, including anorexia (self-starvation) and bulimia (bingeing and purging), are common among teens and younger children. If your step child is developing an eating disorder, you may be the last person to notice. An anorexic's loss of weight may be so gradual you do not notice. Bulimics can maintain a normal weight. Watch to see if she heads to the bathroom right after eating. Eating disorders require professional help, so do not try the do-it-yourself approach

- Substance use is not the same as substance abuse, and kids will experiment in their teen years. When a child or teen is already stressed, however, substance use can easily turn to abuse. Substance abuse is rarely obvious or glaring as trash baskets full of empty gin bottles, track marks on an arm, or scary people tromping through your house bearing syringes and burning all your spoons. Look for other signs: plunging school grades, change in weight, or loss of interest in life. By the time a child is addicted to a substance, there are other visible troubles.

If you are unsure how to approach your step child when you think there is trouble, speak with their biological parent and contact a professional. You do not want things to get out of hand. I knew a family one time who talked about trouble in "another family" as a way of trying to flush out the trouble with their own child. The parents figured by raising an example it would open their communication line to talk about the "what if" and what was happening and should not be. Although it may have worked a couple of times, it is not a reliable method to get information out of your children. Seek professional help or speak with a school counselor to get the correct way to determine if your child or step child is having behavior problems and why.

Homeschooling

The Coronavirus Pandemic of 2020 has caused a lot of parents to homeschool. But many parents have been homeschooling for a long time. Many parents who homeschool, are passionate about their decision to educate their kids in their home environment. However, some parents have been forced to homeschool due to a loss of job or illness.

Legal requirements for homeschooling in the U.S. vary from place to place. Some states have few or no requirements; others ask for portfolio reviews or standardized testing at certain intervals. In almost all areas of the country, parents do not need an education degree to homeschool.

Pros and Cons

There are differences in beliefs when it comes to homeschooling. Many parents choose to homeschool their children because they see the many benefits of homeschooling. Differences in ideology and issues with public school policy are only a few reasons why some parents choose homeschooling over public or private schools. Most colleges are beginning to take note of homeschooling's popularity. Even Ivy League universities have recruited and accepted homeschooled graduates. While there are positive aspects, there are also negative aspects.

Here are 10 potential benefits of homeschooling for parents:
- Continuing education. You can continue to learn alongside your child.
- Save money on school clothes/uniforms and travel to/from school.

- Freedom from school schedule.
- Determine the curriculum.
- Create strong bonds with their children.
- Provide religious and ethical instruction for their children.
- Spend extra time helping their children develop any special talents they possess, including musical, athletic, etc.
- Take children on vacations when public school is still in session.
- Be able to integrate pertinent life skills into the curriculum.
- Adapt teaching methods best suiting how their children learn.

Here are 10 potential disadvantages of homeschooling:
- Spend large amounts of money on books and other learning materials.
- Constantly adapt to be effective teachers, especially when unsure of what you are teaching.
- Constantly motivate their children.
- Be around their children all day.
- Frequently explain their reasons for homeschooling to friends and family with unsympathetic about their decision.
- Restrain anger and remain patient when children struggle with learning.
- How to handle the difficulties at moving at a slower pace than public schooling.
- Lack of social interaction for their children.
- Lack of activities for children to be involved in.
- No personal time.

Homeschooling can be hard on everyone. Many children don't have the patience to sit in front of a laptop for hours on end. Kids can play games online for hours and hours, but not receive educational materials for that long. Frustrating…I know.

Frustration

Many adults get frustrated trying to homeschool due to the following:

- Lack of control. If your children or step children haven't learned to obey you and are out of control, you will be constantly frustrated. Trying to teach them anything academically will be very stressful. You may need to take a short break from the academics and work on the obedience. Be consistent. Discipline and training are not interruptions in your day, but are opportunities to take control and teach them what is considered acceptable behavior.
- Arguing and sibling fights. This is probably the most frustrating items. It can be overwhelming when the kids are continually teasing, bossing, putting each other down, etc. There are daily opportunities to teach each child they are unique. We need to work on teaching them kindness, how to respond to irritations, practice self-control and to deal with sibling rivalry. This is all a part of life.
- Disorganization. Keep school books, paper, or pencils in one spot. Having your kids running around looking for things is distracting. It is well worth it for you to set aside some time to get organized. Make a weekly schedule for everyone to follow, that includes household chores. Keep in mind that a schedule is a tool only. It's a way to incorporate your priorities and goals into each day, and accomplish the things that matter. Allow for flexibility as needed. A written schedule also teaches organizations skills to your children.
- Unrealistic Expectations. Do you put a lot of unnecessary pressure on yourself and expect more than what is truly realistic?

This can stem from comparison. Don't allow yourself to compare what you are doing to what someone else is doing. It's also common to get frustrated because we are unrealistic in what we expect from our kids. It's important to remember that each child is different, and have different learning styles and abilities. Because of this, we need to be realistic in our expectations with each child, saving ourselves from a lot of frustration. Life is busy, and we all face the challenge of having to choose which things to say yes to, and saying no to a lot more things than we say yes to. We can't do it all.

In thinking about the pros and cons, and the frustrations involved, now throw in the mix the complication of dealing with a step child. All of this may be too overwhelming for a step-parent to take on. Just know your options and secure a backup plan. Enlist the neighbor's help who might be homeschooling their children. Work as a community instead of bearing the burden alone.

Teenagers: What to Expect

Dealing with Your Adolescent Step Child

You can make life around your household easier if you try the following:

- Do not take it personally. Think of your step-teen as hormonally impaired. Try to be tolerant, and give it time.
- Do not try to compare or compete with the other biological parent. Be more yourself than you have ever been in your life.
- Spend time alone with your step-teen doing activities which interest you both.
- Be neutral about your partner's ex-spouse. If provoked by the step-teen about him, take five deep breaths and take the high road.
- Do not push for affection, attention, or response.

Encourage your partner to follow these steps:

- Reassure him will never abandon him emotionally or physically, and no one (meaning you) will ever come between the two of them.
- Spend time alone with his kids doing things they like to do, such as talking together and playing games.
- Occasionally side with the kids against you and, also occasionally, let you and your step child side with each other. (United fronts are important, but let it be a front, not a brick wall.)

Your partner should let you and your step child work out your own disagreements. Both of you can help matters by following these pointers:

- Your step child is sensitive in his new body and hormone-laden mind. Try not to nag. Write notes on paper or text them.
- Let Go. You are looking for balance here, giving more autonomy while remaining involved in their life. Children need room, but also need guidance and interest.
- Show you care. Kids will treat you as if they do not care, but show you care anyway. Do not be put off by the seeming indifference.
- Be aware of transitional periods. The coming-and-going transitions can be worse with teenagers than with younger children, simply because teens tend to be moodier anyway. Give them time and space to adjust.

Discipline and the Step-teen

Adolescents thrive on the balance of caring and positive discipline, but things are complicated by this step business. It takes a long time for a teenager to respect a step-parent's authority.

- Go slow. Build rapport before asserting your authority.
- Talk about it. Verbal communication is an important aspect of discipline.
- Hands off! If it needs to be handled, let the biological parent do it. Discipline should always be lighter for teenagers than for younger children. Allow consequences to be as natural as possible. Let them demonstrate what was learned.

- No scolding. Voicing disapproval does not work. Teens are not dumb. Teenagers know what will happen if they don't study or do whatever is required of them. Show them the respect of letting him make his own decisions, and live with the consequences (so long as no one is in physical danger.)

Temptations

Kids are exposed to temptations of sex, drugs, and alcohol everywhere, at almost all ages. By the time your step child is thirteen, she is already making decisions about becoming involved with chemical substances. Sex rears its head early, too. If you are not familiar with teenagers, it may shock you what he is like, what he is into, and what he is exposed to. Get familiar with what is out there. Know the risks and the dangers.

Step-teen Advantages

There can be wonderful advantages to being the step-parent of a teenager. Teens desperately need adult allies who are not their biological parents. If you play your cards right, you can be the confidante, the other grown-up, the understanding one when the biological parents do not have a clue. The same teenager who is so mean to parents they want to turn her in for a new model often shows her real charm, enthusiasm, compassion, and fresh view of life to other adults. This could be you. Just be careful of that fine line of "friendship." We already discussed you aren't friends. They have enough friends.

Knowledge goes a long way. Understanding what teens are normally like will help you understand when your step-teen is having problems. Here are a few misconceptions:

- Teens are awful, thoughtless, and impossible.
- Teens from "broken" families get messed up with sex, drugs, and criminal elements.
- The stress of a step family added to the normal stresses of adolescence lead to depression, eating disorders, and suicide.

Here are the realities:

- Adolescence is a time of stress, and, yes, your step-teen may be awful and cruel at times. A new step family does not make it easier (but may not make it harder, either).
- Adolescents can be charming, warm, caring, and interesting to be around. It is a joy to watch them come into their own self.
- Teenagers do not want an adversarial relationship any more than step-parents do.
- Rebellion is part of being a teenager, and your step-teen is not necessarily going to be more messed up than another teenager.
- What matters is not the structure of the family, but the quality of it.

The Hormone Years

Teenagers are beautiful, angry, sexual, sassy, messy, moody, and often lethargic. Hormonal changes (moodiness, lethargy, and so on) begin about two years before the outward physical changes can be seen.

Respect the moods of a teen. Can you imagine it? Do you remember it? It's hard being a teenager. Not only is your body betraying you by sprouting all this hair and growing in peculiar ways, but there is school and work pressure, and pressure of what you are going to do with the rest of your life. If all teens have it bad (and all teens do according to them), the step-teen has an added stress: a new step family to get deal with. A moody teenager needs room to simply exist, and he also needs you to offer to talk about it. Do active listening, but do not push.

Teenagers need privacy: time alone, private space, and private thoughts. Respect this need and do not pry. Knock on a closed door and wait for an answer before entering. (Remember your core family values.) Do not ever read a teens' journal. You will be sorry, and if you are found out, you will break the trust between the two of you forever and ever and ever...

The Humiliation Factor

All parents, not particularly step-parents, are embarrassing. You are so uncool. Your clothes are out of style. Need I continue? Do not feel too insulted when your step-teen makes you drop her off around the corner from her intended spot because you are driving a less than cool car instead of an awesome one.

Moving in with the Other Biological Parent

It's fairly common for a teen that lived primarily with one parent for years to want to change households and live with the other parent. Part of this is the adolescent's quest for identity and trying on new roles and new lifestyles. Part of it could be it is not always easy for a teen and a teen's parents to get along. Household shifting is especially common when a boy has been living with his mom and wants to be in closer contact with his dad, a male role model. As a step-parent, be prepared for a sudden change in your lifestyle. You may have a live-in step child without notice, or all at once you may find yourself with far less children in your daily life.

Adult Step Children

Bonding

If the step children are adults, the immediate day-to-day issues of step-parenting will not feel as pressing. However, if you are a step-parent to adults your own age (or older), other issues may apply. It is up to the biological parent to assert you as his partner and equal.

As the step-parent of an adult step child who is your age or older, keep these things in mind:

- You may have a problem being taken seriously as a person and as the biological parent's partner.
- Your motives may be looked on with suspicion.
- If you have moved into the family house, you may have difficulty asserting yourself as an adult.
- The adult step child may stereotype the relationship and you: "She is looking for a father figure" or "He wants a sugar-mama."
- Your partner's child may feel threatened his territory is taken over by the relationship.
- You may have to deal with increased sexual tension between you and the adult step child.
- You may run into generation gap issues. Where do you belong?
- Legal issues such as wills, powers-of-attorney, and so on may become more of an issue.
- You have the potential for a rewarding friendship.

When people get overwhelmed, most tend to withdraw and become resentful. Part of making the transition and commitment to step-parenting involves making a firm attempt to know each of your step children individually, and apart from your partner. Like other step children, it may take time, work, and respect for the adult step child to come around.

Keep this in mind:

- Having a relationship with your adult step children will not happen overnight so go slowly. Having a short conversation may seem worthless, but it is not. Every positive interaction you have with them sets the next one up to be better and possibly longer.
- Insist on being respected. Adult step children can behave badly and feel loyalty to their absent parent or feel, because the adults are grown up, they do not need to have a relationship with you at all. Explain to them disrespecting you is disrespecting your partner and the decision he/she has made.
- Be polite and civil. Just be aware the adult step children may not return being polite or civil.
- Listen to them. Part of creating a relationship with adult step children is making them think their lives are important to you. Ask questions about their day but do not get too personal.
- Be a friend, not a parent. I know I have told you about not being a step child's friend, but with an adult it is not the same. An adult step child does not need another parent. He already has at least one, often two, and is capable of running his own life. Listen to him as a friend would, but do not attempt to tell him what to do.

- Let your adult step children have alone time with your partner. Remember, they were a part of this family before you came along. Be respectful and allow them to have time.
- Understand your adult step children may not always be open about their feelings, but, even if they behave oddly, they do still want to be liked and admired by you.
- Laugh. A sense of humor can alleviate potentially difficult situations and can create a feeling of closeness between you, if both you and your step children can see the funny side of things.
- Communicate. Even if it feels like things are always going to be difficult, do not stop trying to make them better. Tell your step children how you feel, what you think could help solve a difficult situation and, most importantly, let them know you like them.

Solo Outings

Here is an approach: Try the solo outing. Getting to know them one-on-one is an important part of building a relationship.

- Make it an activity with part of, but not all, the focus on each other. This is not an encounter session; it is an outing.
- Do an activity fun for both of you, not too expensive, but definitely make sure to pick up the bill.
- Do not believe everything you hear. Be open in the communication lines. If he tells you something in confidence, then respect his wishes no matter how much you want to tell your partner. I am not encouraging you to keep secrets from your partner, but in order to build a relationship (as long as no one is getting hurt), then you should consider his request.
- Do not ask "How's school or work?" Forget your parental role, and hang out.

- Work on feeling comfortable with silence. You may not have anything to say to each other. Concentrate on relaxing.
- Make it a regular thing. A one-time outing doesn't work. So, what if you do not have instant chemistry together. A relationship requires work, time, and more time.

Small Steps

Relationships are built through shared experiences, and solo outings are a way to begin putting in the time. If there is a negative reaction to the idea try not to feel rejected. Fight the bitterness. Now is the time to practice your long-term perspective. The key is to:

- Invite him again. And again. And chances are eventually he will give in and attend an outing with you.
- Stop taking things so personal. Relax.
- Don't give up.

Finding a Home

When step families begin discussing living situations, past living arrangements and money issues often come up, especially when couples who have uneven financial situations come together as a family. Perhaps she lived in a middle-class house in the suburbs with a pool and a large mortgage, and he is fresh from a small urban rent-controlled apartment downtown. How much rent or mortgage can you afford? How much do you want to afford?

The couple could try to find a place where each can afford half of the housing costs, or could approach it another way. Each could figure out how much one can contribute individually and then decide what the couple can afford. As long as everyone is happy, it does not need to be 50/50. Keep the lines of communication open to prevent resentments from building up. Make sure each one is comfortable with what the other can commit to. You do not want this to come up later in arguments when one might say "I own most of this house so you have to do what I say."

When Not to Move

There are times in each child's life where a change, such as moving to another community or city, can be devastating. Most times it is a young child who needs the security of their family home and school. It might be a teenager who wants to finish high school with friends. You may want to reconsider your plans. Perhaps when you think about it, the parent who has the child living with them full time should stay put, and the step-parent (with no children or with only visiting children) should move in. It doesn't hurt to try this, especially if you need to save money to afford a larger home.

Moving in with Your Partner

When you (and your kids, if you have them) move into an already established household, you come in as a third wheel. Never mind you were invited or are there by mutual consent. You will still have to deal with this issue of claiming the home as your own without appearing to be an intruder.

Incorporate the "old" furniture into a new look. Mix `n' match. Buy new sofa covers, new throw rugs or lamps to give the place a new look. You cannot erase the past, so combine it with the present and move on into the future.

Claiming Your Space

Claiming space is touchy, especially if you or your partner is literally displacing a family member. Go slow. Wildly redecorating the entire house will feel like an emotional challenge to the step children, and possibly to your partner. You might want to shift bedrooms around, or at least reorganize the furniture, especially if this is a home where the ex-partner lived when the first family was all together. By making small changes it could make a world of difference for comfort for everyone. No one wants to compete with memories from the past.

Defeating Ghosts

If the ex-partner is deceased, the family might take your reorganizing and redecorating personally. Be prepared for the children to react. You do not have to live with the objects of a deceased one's life. Tell your partner you need support on this issue. Enlist the kids to help you pack the belongings. If the children are not ready to sort and dispose of the effects, invest in a small storage rental unit until they are. Know this process could take two to three years for them to be comfortable disposing of them.

When Your Partner Moves in with You

If you have young children who crawl into bed with you in the middle of the night, discuss how you are going to handle this with your new partner. For personal stuff, create an "off-limits" area—a room, a corner of a room, a desk, or a bookshelf—where you can keep the stuff you do not want tampered with and you do not want to put into storage. And be prepared to have it be a tempting spot for kids.

Perhaps you are the one with the larger home and everyone is joining you. If you do not have kids of your own, be prepared for an adjustment period as you learn to live with young ones. Are you prepared for fingerprints on the white drapes, cracked dishes, and piles of damp towels on the bathroom floor?

You have to let go. Do not be so attached to your possessions, or put them in storage. Put the expensive china high on the shelf and invest in playful plastic tumblers.

Coming to Terms on Furniture

What is tradition, comfort, and classic taste to some is old, putrid, and worn-out to others. Yes, you may love each other, but you may hate each other's choice in home decorations. Relationships have broken up—all over furniture. Furniture and other furnishings reflect who all of you are, survivors of your lives so far, bringing your history and past with you.

At times, hostility toward items is misplaced hostility toward people. Do you really hate your stepson's "heavy metal band" poster, or are you flinging it wildly into the trash because you resent how he has been ignoring you?

Post-Move Syndrome

A new place will not fix everything. Moving is traumatic and expensive, and when everyone has to move, someone will be traumatized. Yes, the new house may have fresh clean paint, but those moving into it are still the people from before. After the movers are gone, you may find yourselves standing around and looking at each other thinking "now what?" Post-Move Syndrome Letdown (PMSL) is common. Hang in there and try to enjoy setting up your new household. Make sure to include everyone on the set up.

Establishing Your Own Family Style

Part of becoming a family is forming your own family style. At first, it will feel like a combination of two broken sets, but slowly you will add new things, perhaps in a new style.

Since it is the kids' house too, you want to include the children in the decorating decisions. This helps them to feel valued and will give you another way to get to know each other. Listen to the child's needs and tastes. It also provides opportunities for two important activities:

- Education. You may know this is an antique chair, but for the step child it is an old ugly chair - until you teach about the distinguishing signs.
- Shared activities. Shop together at flea markets, auctions, or estate sales for old furniture. Refinish or repaint the old dresser. The step child will feel more a part of the process and enjoy using the item he worked on.

Once you are finished decorating, throw a party and celebrate your new look. By celebrating you are showing the children that you love and respect their help and everyone can enjoy the new home.

Cross-Cultural Step Families

Understanding the Culture

As in same culture families, whenever you have a relationship in a cross-cultural situation, you have to make sure to communicate effectively. Intercultural communication requires things such as: respect, tolerance, flexibility, empathy, patience, and humor.

- Respect - One of the biggest complaints by people from non-dominant cultures is lack of respect. You will find by trying to understand and learn about the differences between your culture and your step family's culture will lead to increased respect and improved cross-cultural communication. Try to learn about your step family's culture in specific ways. You can read and research, ask questions, or maybe even learn the language.

- Tolerance - Behavior can mean more than one thing, depending upon what culture the person is from. There are differences in language, style, and behavior. When an African-American child looks at you and says "You're bad," she may not be saying you are a naughty step-parent. An Asian-American child's refusal to look an adult in the eye will be interpreted as shifty in some cultures, but merely respectful in his.

- Flexibility – You will do best in life when you remain flexible, particularly in situations new or challenging. Here is where your self-awareness of your own values steps in again. If you understand yourself, you will be able to relax when things are going worse than expected, as long as it does not threaten your real values.

- Empathy - Feeling what another person feels, and walking a mile in his shoes is important for cross-cultural communication. Try feeling what a person might be feeling in new or strange surroundings. It may give you a whole new perspective on the world.

- Patience - Cross-cultural communication (and living in a cross-cultural step family) can be difficult. Be patient. Family growth takes time.

- Humor - Miscommunications can be funny but it can also be hurtful. Laughter is essential in a family when you have to learn new customs and learn to live with a whole bunch of new strangers. When you lose your sense of humor, you can lose your perspective. Make sure when you laugh, you are laughing with them and not at them.

Your cross-cultural communication will be improved by your willingness to know yourself and to understand your reactions. Your perceptions of the world and your values affect your interpretation of what other people are saying and doing. You have to understand yourself and what you are bringing to the step family (good points, old baggage, values, expectations, and beliefs) to understand the others.

Differences in Cultures

Americans tend to be informal and tend to shake each other's hands. Other cultures may be more formal and use hugs, kisses and handshakes in their greetings. You may think your stepdaughter is walking behind you because she is embarrassed to be seen with you, but she might be showing you respect—in some cultures, it is a way of honoring you.

Cultures differ in their sense of personal space. People from northern European cultures like to stand further away than people from southern European cultures. If you are in a step family with people from a more southern area, people may (wrongly) consider you cold or uncaring because you are not as willing to invade personal space like them.

You are My Family

Even the perceptions of friends and family can differ between cultures.

- The dominant American culture tends to focus on the nuclear family. In other cultures, the family unit is the extended family— uncles, aunts, cousins, and their best friends from grade school.
- Loyalties are another story.
- Self-responsibility is highly valued in different cultures. In others, people believe more in their loyalty and responsibility to their family.
- In some cultures, the elderly is given status and respect. Not true everywhere though.

A strong family identity is a foundation for everyone in the family to stand on. Building a family identity is more than a matter of deciding on the family rules and family style. A family also has a sense of shared history. In a step family, you will want to build your history through shared experiences.

In a cross-cultural family, you need to do more. You need to learn about your step family's culture and teach them about yours. As you build your family identity, your customs and background may be incorporated into your step children' lives, becoming a part of their own sense of history, continuity, and future. However, do not try and force your culture on them.

Here are tips for letting them know who you are.

- Teach them your language - Language is culture. Teach your step children your language, or at least give them a taste. Learn their language. This includes their slang.
- Invite your step children into your community - A White-American child may have no idea of the beauty of a gospel church in full swing. An African-American child may be blown away at your family's annual reunion.
- Cook for them or take them out to eat – The children may not be familiar with the types of foods you eat, nor you be familiar with theirs, but trying each other's foods is a great start. It may take time to adjust - do not force the issue. Do not make the children eat what they do not want, but explain why your culture enjoys those types of foods.
- Play them your music – As we all know; musical taste differs from culture to culture and person to person and generation to generation. What one person likes the other may not. By telling them what you like to listen to lets them know more about you. Make sure to give them the same courtesy.
- Share personal stories with them – Stories are a great way to get to know people. Sharing stories of your culture and how you grew up will help them to understand you more.

How to Communicate (Remember Active Listening?)

- Speak Slow and Simple - Use simple words, short sentences, and enunciate. Do not use slang. And, do not assume she understand what you said when you said it because you said it. If there is even the slightest of a doubt about understanding, ask her to repeat back to you what you said.

- Listen to them – Listen to what he is saying and do not correct his grammar. Listen for the positive intent. Do not judge. After he speaks, wait before responding. Watch for cues in facial expression, gestures and body language before replying.
- Ask for more information – You want to make sure you understand each other. Do not assume smiling and nodding means she understood or agrees.
- Give instructions – Make sure to give step-by-step instructions, but do not explain all of the steps at once. Ask if he has any questions and be ready (and happy) to answer them. Ask him to repeat back what he understood.

Nonverbal Communication Skills

Gestures do not always have the same meaning in some cultures and ethnic groups. Try to become aware of cultural taboos, such as: Do not put your hand on a Thai child's head and do not point your chopsticks at someone from Japan. These are both insulting gestures. In some cultures, touching may not be acceptable. In others, walking with arms around each other, holding hands, or hugging between members of the same sex is expected. Eye contact can be interpreted as a challenge, a sign of disrespect, or the sign of an honest, forthright person, depending on what culture you come from.

Adjusting to Differences

With differences in values, lifestyle, and approaches to child-rearing, you and your partner will have communicating and problem-solving to do.

Because the differences and conflicts are visible in cross-cultural step families, you are more likely to put in the time and energy to get to know and respect each other's ways. Doing this increases your chances of having a well-blended step family.

Food and Dietary Restrictions

Where there are dietary restrictions, whether for religious or moral reasons, it is vital to respect them. Never serve meat on a vegetarian's plate and force him to eat. It is cruel and disrespectful. Respect has to go both ways. You may end up having several sets of pots and pans (one for meat, one for dairy products, and one for the non-kosher vegetarian), but at least you will have mutual respect in the household.

Families often have conflicts over how much to eat and whether a child should be forced to clean his plate. It is a challenge for most of us to relax, to present healthy food, and to let children regulate their own intake. People of all cultures should realize food is not an area you can effectively regulate. Setting boundaries and limits around your child's eating patterns will only lead you to trouble. Do not cause yourself extra stress here. Let it go. When kids are hungry, they will eat.

Religious Differences

Interfaith families are increasingly common, and not just in step families. One may convert to the other person's religion. Or, Mom and Dad try to raise the kids with both religions. Parents have been known to throw up their hands and give up on official worship, and others split down the middle and have two camps.

You may want to talk with your spiritual leader or pastor about solutions for interfaith challenges. Many organized religions run interfaith groups and classes. No matter what approach you take to religion, it is essential other people's religious choices be respected. You will not have much of a marriage (or a family) if essential beliefs and moral values are disrespected. We will dive more into how religion can be a big part of how your family comes together in another chapter.

Socioeconomic Differences

Culture is not a matter of what country your people come from, or what religion you practice. Socioeconomic differences, if they exist, can lead to unique approaches to living. It is not a matter of how much money you make, it can include the values around how you talk about and spend money, your attitudes toward credit, your upbringing and manners, your family's emphasis on education, and more. Understanding is the key to tolerance.

No Matter What

No matter what religion you are, what socioeconomic background you have, or where you came from, it is important to give each other respect and space. Everyone was not made from the same mold - thank goodness. Hang in there and find a way to enjoy the differences.

Grandparents

Grandparents and grandchildren may form a tight unit and exclude everyone else. This often happens with the "other" grandparents, a.k.a. the ex-partner's parents. Most parents will side with their own child in a divorce, and have been known to encourage their grandkids to look at the new step-parent as the intruder. But it can also happen with the grandparents. If your step children are having a hard time with the situation or with you, the doting grandparents (your loving partner's parents) may side with the children against you. Of course, by doing this, grandparents are siding against their own child's choice of a partner, which should not happen.

Measuring Up

Being measured against the ex-partner does not always mean you will come out looking bad. But any type of measuring is not fair. One may feel never fully accepted into the family. People will be polite but make no special effort to welcome you into the family. The children's loyalty can be swayed (for no reason).

Morality and Judgment

Values and morality can get between the older and younger generations. It is painful when your parents, the step grandparents, disown you and ignore your step children because you married a divorced person, or when the grandparents take the side of the ex-partner (particularly ex-wives) and disown their own child. It does happen. Many people cannot be convinced of the validity and importance of your step family. When this happens, it is a tremendous loss to all.

Biological and Non-Biological Grandchildren

Combined families can get complicated. If you marry a person with one child and you have one child, the grandparents of the biological child may only bring them gifts. Is it fair? Of course not, but before this happens you should to sit down with the grandparents to let them know this type of behavior will be unacceptable. While you cannot expect step grandparents to care as much about their step grandchildren and the step siblings of their grandchildren, grandparents do need to show courtesy and respect to your family unit. It is up to you and your partner to assert yourself in these matters and to request equal treatment.

Step Children Ignoring Step Grandparents

It can be the other way around, your parents are a dream, but your step children are being difficult. If the kids are being overly cold to your parents, the kids might not realize it is okay not to love them. The child may have picked up a complaint against them from you or your partner, or may be worried about betraying their own grandparents. They will pout and ignore.

Here is assistance:

- Reassure the child he does not have to love or even like your parents. But he must be respectful.
- Increase familiarity by telling them about each parent. Seek shared interests or character traits.

- On the other hand, if your step children are being rude to your parents (or to their grandparents or other grandparents), it is time for a talk. We all know kids can be cruel, and difficult. If it is not respectful, it is not acceptable. Reinforce this.

Other Grandparents and You

The other grandparents are still a part of your step children's family, and will always be even if the ex-partner is deceased. You may never meet these people; the other grandparents might act neutral, or might be mean and try to poison your step children against you. You can try to resolve problems, or you can let it slide, hoping, once again, truth, justice, and the step-parent way will win out. Whatever you do, remember you cannot divorce the children from their grandparents, even if your partner has no relationship with those grandparents anymore.

Remember the obvious: Half of your step kids' grandparents are the parents of the ex-partner—they are the "other" grandparents. Their loyalties lie with the ex-partner, and should, and may see you as a challenge. Be welcoming. Do not damage or limit their relationship with their grandchildren.

If you and your partner have custody of the children, the other grandparents may feel cast aside, not considered, and sad about the loss of their grandkids. It is important for the kids to be able to maintain a relationship with all their grandparents. Offer them a visitation schedule. Be the better person here for the children's sake. If you don't want to have personal contact with them, suggest taking the kids out alone. If you are open-minded, you might include them in a family event or holiday.

It may feel odd at first, inviting the parents of your partner's ex over, say, for dinner. There are no rules about what is right or wrong. You need to go by your own comfort level. While you will never feel comfortable hanging out with the ex-partner's parents, most people are decent and will rise to the occasion in particular cases.

Conflicts between All the Grandparents

Rivalry is not just about siblings. Grandparents can get competitive with each other, and because there are several sets of grandparents in a step family situation, the squabbles can get extensive. Steer clear and avoid taking sides. If it gets too horrendous, then the solution is to call a therapist for you and maybe for the kids. Talk with the kids to make sure everything is okay. Assure them you care about them.

Separation Is a Last Resort

Grandparents are so important to kids, and kids are so important to grandparents. It is imperative to try to work out all problems. Much of the burden here is on you. You need to be explicit about what behavior is needed from everyone involved.

Grandparents may not be a great influence on the kids, and may say nasty things about you and your family, and may have other beliefs and try to impose those on the children. Take a leap of faith—you have tremendous influence on your step children. This influence may be challenged, but it is not threatened, by the grandparents. The world is abundant with people who have other things to offer. All you can do is teach kids your own values the best way you can and then let them go.

Other tips:

- Do not feel left out of the family dynamics. This may mean you have to resist the urge to mope in the corner. Enlist your partner's help.
- Do not push friendship into your relationship with either set of grandparents. For a while, consider them your step children' grandparents. You cannot expect instant friendship. Give it time.
- If you think things are going terribly, you might need to consider having a family meeting to reinforce what is expected from all family members. Include the grandparents in the meeting. We are all adults and should act as such.
- Again, as a last resort, you should consider a separation period. This is not recommended, but there are times when everyone needs a time out.

The Rights of Grandparents

Grandparents do not have many legal rights, though some have a few. In certain states, the Courts can grant visitation rights to grandparents. But just because the grandparent petitions it doesn't mean he will win. It has to be in the best interest of the child. There are times when the grandparents have to prove having a deep and lasting relationship with the grandchild. The grandparents may gain visitation if the child lived with them for a while. And other times the Courts will turn them down, saying recognizing their rights would compromise the parents' rights of choosing with whom their children can associate.

Here is some information on the other grandparents' rights when their grandkids are adopted by a step-parent. Each state has their set of rules and regulations. Make sure to consult with an attorney for verification.

- Normally step-parent adoption removes all ties between the adopted child and their biological family, and other grandparents. The Courts have granted visitation rights to other grandparents in step-parent adoption in a few cases. Other grandparents have the best chance for visitation when the step-parent adoption follows the death of their child and parent of the grandchild (rather than relinquishment or abandonment).

Wills

Step grandparents must be explicit in their wills if their desire is to have their step-grandchildren to inherit from them after their death. Make sure to consult with an attorney on the proper way to complete and file a Will.

The Grandparent during the Divorce

Grandparents are commonly called upon to bail out the parents during a divorce by taking care of the children. In hard times, grandparents can provide an anchoring influence. In other times, the anchor is dislodged when the parent remarries and reclaims the child.

When the child moves from Grandma and Grandpa's house to the new household with her parent and new step-parent, the grandparents can easily feel displaced or unappreciated. If you are the step-parent in a situation like this, be aware the other grandparents may take out their hostility on you. Make sure you and your partner express your appreciation and your respect for them. Make it your job to build bridges – not burn them.

The Grandparent as Step-parent

Did you know more than three million children in the United States live with their grandparents or other kin, not their parents? Thank God for grandparents giving these children a place to go other than foster care or another state system.

Frequently, grandparents are becoming step-parents to their children's children if the parent is too young to be a responsible, full-time parent. Often it happens when a parent wants to give up a child for adoption and the grandparent will not stand for it. Other times, a parent gets into trouble with drugs or crime or may become incarcerated, and cannot take care of the child.

Grandparents who parent their grandchildren have other complications:

- The relationship with their child is often damaged, strained, or nonexistent. Many grandparents do not want (or actively fear) contact or involvement from the birth parent.
- There is only a small amount of legal assistance for relatives who take on a relative's child.
- Grandparents may also have health complications due to age. (Chasing a toddler when you have had a cardiac by-pass is no walk in the park.)
- Resentment comes with the territory. It is hard to raise a whole new family when you expected to be finished with these responsibilities by now.

The Step as Grandparent

When a step-parent becomes a step-grandparent, things often shift for the better. A new baby tends to bring a family together, and when your step children have children, they often gain a sudden understanding of how challenging step-parenting (all parenting) can be. There is a tremendous amount of joy when a baby begins to recognize you. It is great to see things and situations come full circle. You may even see a little appreciation at this point. Embrace it and enjoy the moment.

Extended Family

More People, More Time, More Decisions

To extend means to enlarge and to reach out. An extended family is both larger and more encompassing of other people.

The size and shape of the American family is changing, becoming more inclusive, more diverse, and more extended. Shared custody (both legal and physical) is becoming more the norm, and unlike in the past, when biological fathers left the scene, more biological dads are often involved in parenting their kids after a divorce. More involvement means more adults in parenting roles and far more well-combined families.

The only problem with this improved state of affairs is the more people there are involved in the activity, the more time it takes to plan things and to negotiate through differences of opinion.

The Value of the Extended Family

Children need other people. Whether they realize it or not, children have a support network of people, including relatives, adult friends, teachers, pastors and members of the community.

In a community, you do not get to choose who lives there. You also do not get to pick your partner's ex-spouse or their family. Nonetheless, all of these people are a distinct part of your community now. Recognize them as part of your step child's (and therefore your) support network, and you are part of theirs. The more you are able to see the big picture and accept the abundance and diversity of this network, the easier it will be for you to rise above individual disagreements.

A working, respectful relationship does not mean beer dates, bowling, or heart-to-hearts with the ex-partner. Your stepdaughter's soccer coach is also involved in your community, but you do not feel compelled to borrow tools or other items from him? Work on developing a practical partnership with the ex-partner, not a close friendship.

Be the Better Person

If things are heating up toward an all-out war, or if the Cold War has been going on for a while, it may be up to you to begin the peace process. Take a deep breath, count to ten and begin.

If things are difficult, start by writing a letter to the other biological parent to break the ice. You could do this over the phone or in person, but it is easier and makes more of an impression when it is on paper. Leave out the name calling and other offensive remarks and get to the heart of the matter. Do whatever is best for the children involved.

Honoring Original Relationships

Combining and extending is fantastic, but it is important to continue to honor the original relationship between biological parent and biological child. If you are a biological parent, spend special time alone with your own child.

Let the child know:

- You are there for them.

- You are not trying to take over the parenting role.
- You will put aside disagreements and put their interests first.
- You will make yourself available to talk or correspond any time she has anything to discuss.

Think how much easier your life would be if you didn't have burning anxiety every time you or your partner had to deal with the ex-partner.

The Other Relatives

How the family of your partner's ex-partner feels about you will depend, in part, on how and why your partner's previous relationship broke up.

What about your step children's aunts, uncles, cousins, second cousins, and third-cousins-twice-removed? Your partner's ex-partners relatives may be a part of your new family network.

Here is another opportunity to grow your community and incorporate more concerned adults into your extended family. Once again, it may be up to you to take the first step and be the better person, especially if your partner's past relationship ended in disaster.

Setting Realistic Goals

In your step-parenting endeavors, it is vital to keep your expectations in check and to set reasonable goals for yourself and for your step family.

If you try for perfection, you are doomed to fail. Do the best you can, and be patient. Change takes time.

When you do set goals, be prepared to make changes along the way. Cut large goals into smaller ones to have wins along the way.

Guilt can be Destructive

Guilt can be a destructive force to you and to others. But guilt can be a positive force when it reminds us that we always have the opportunity to improve ourselves and our actions.

We all get defensive when reading a self-help book and it points out things you have done wrong and suggests ways of doing things you haven't tried yet. Never let guilt over your past step-parenting practice get to you. Do not beat yourself up. It is never too late to make changes, and it is never too late to improve your step relationships.

Intrusive Ex-Partners

There can be times when the ex-partner is too much of a fixture in your life. If this feels like a problem to either you or your partner, look closely at what is going on. Perhaps one of them is still not over the relationship. Insist on separation. If your partner is having trouble with this, get help. A couple of sessions with a counselor may make a noticeable difference. You are not number two because your love and commitment came after the ex-partner's love and commitment.

It could be you, too, are having a hard time with your own ex, if you have one. Divorced couples go through three stages: holding on, letting go, and starting over. The ex-partners reach these stages at different times. Just because you and your partner are over it, your ex-partner may not be. Many people feel it would be easier to let go and start over if each one didn't have to see the other. Unfortunately, when you have children, this is not always possible.

Death of an Ex-Partner

Even when the ex-partner has died, your partner will need to complete the separation process of holding on, letting go, and starting over to fully let go of the relationship.

At times the ex-partner will intrude on her ex-partner after the death of their partner. This can cause a rift between the married couple. Once a person is single the sympathy card is played, making it difficult for the other partner to move on.

Stand firm and do not enable the ex-partner get in-between you and your partner. This will in turn help them to move on quicker and to be able to fend for themselves. Suggest counseling if you feel your ex-partner is too dependent on you.

Badmouthing – Bad Idea

Dealing with a nasty biological parent who is saying awful things about you to the kids provides you with a brilliant opportunity: You get to be the good step-parent! Model positive behavior to the kids, keep them from running wild, and refrain from badmouthing the parent.

The telephone is intrusive. When you pick up the phone, you run the risk of hearing your sweetheart's ex-partner on the other end. Take three deep breaths and blow off the negative energy. Do not let it ruin your mood. And do not vent to the rest of the family.

Badmouthing a biological parent (even if the parent is absent, abusive or rude) will backfire on you. You can and will affect the child and their self-esteem if you tell them their biological parent has issues. The children will always defend the biological parent, thereby causing a setback in the relationship between you and them. Do not badmouth the ex. If you are guilty of doing this, stop. If you are tempted to do it – don't.

Children of divorce understand their biological parents' good sides and their bad sides, but do not as a rule, draw the conclusions an outsider would make from those records. No matter what you say, (or do not say), you have to let the children assess the other parent for themselves and come to the conclusions on their own. Fortunately, later in life, young adults have a way of looking back and knowing who took the best care of them. Sit back, relax, and be the positive role model we talked about before.

There is NO Competition

You cannot fix what was wrong with your partner's previous relationship, and you cannot make yourself into a better match. All you can do is be yourself and work to make your relationship the best you can. It can be a temptation to learn all you can about the ex-partner, but do not go there. It is not going to improve your relationship and it will only make you crazy.

Be aware: ex-partners have a great working relationship when each is single, but the moment one of them has a new partner, then there is a new person in the mix, and the replacement tends to bring out the worst in people.

If you are a woman with the same last name as the first Mrs., you may have a few uncomfortable experiences as you are mistaken for each other. It can be uncomfortable being the second anything. Hyphen your name if it will make you feel better, but first discuss this with your partner. Do not let things get to you. You are number one in your new partner's eyes.

Planning Holidays

A step-parent who has particular holiday traditions from the rest of the family, especially a step-parent with no child of their own, can feel left out of the celebration. All family traditions have force. It is vital for everyone to be considered when planning holidays.

Things you should consider when planning holidays:

- Who is going to spend the holiday where? Holiday plans can be predetermined by custody or shared parental agreements. If you have the flexibility of options, discuss them with the children and try to be flexible around their desires. Some families split up the holidays each year. "I'll take Halloween and you take Thanksgiving," or some try to do both "I'll take Christmas Eve (Mom) and "I'll take Christmas Day" (Dad). Several people celebrate twice, once with each parent. You also need to consider where the gifts will be opened. Parents who purchase gifts for their children like to see their reactions when the child is opening the gift. How would you feel if you didn't get to see their surprise? Make sure you think of all parties involved when making plans.
- Take into account the religions of those involved. Hanukkah and Christmas for example. It is important to keep family traditions alive with certain cultures.
- Watch out for trouble on the step sibling front when the kids have other plans. Step children can feel left out if there are "whole" kids in the picture. (Remember your new baby!) Try to

keep the presents even, and have the major festivities take place when all the kids are present.

- Create New Holidays - If all the holidays seem to be taken up with stress and other people's claims ("But Thanksgiving is mine!"), you can always select another day (Cinco de Mayo, Arbor Day, Step-parents Day) to become an annual blow-out holiday. Give gifts. Decorate the house. Throw a party!

- If you will not have the children for the holiday, create an alternate festivity for yourselves. Do not stay home and mope. Do not force false cheer. Make new memories. Get creative.

- Plan ahead. Do not let expectations go unspoken otherwise you will be doomed to disappointment.

- The first few years, try to lower your expectations.

- Do not assume holidays will be calm and peaceful if daily life is full of conflict. There is no holiday from mixed feelings, and you cannot force fun, laughter and family spirit.

- Do not expect holidays to be as you had in the past. Also be aware the loss of the old ways of doing things is a disappointment for the kids, and for you.

- Discuss how holidays were for each of you, and have each person define which rituals are most important to them. This can be hard to hear but it is important. Incorporate into your holidays a few of these important old rituals.

- The winter holidays are traditionally a time of family togetherness. You and your partner can have private time too but always take the children and step children into consideration.

- Acknowledge you are starting from scratch. There is a new excitement about having the opportunity to create holidays as you would like them to be. Then create a few new family rituals or traditions, things none of you have done before. Aim for creating your own holiday spirit (with additions) and welcoming kids into it.

- Do not try to re-create another's rituals. You cannot make it as it was, you do not want it as it was, and you will only make people unhappy if you try. It will definitely backfire.
- Be flexible and encourage flexibility.
- If things are tense, do not force get-togethers, or minimize the amount of time spent together.
- Remember to celebrate. You are a real family.

Adult Step children and the Holiday Season

The more adults in the family, the more confusion and chaos there is in terms of holiday logistics. When step children partner up and start their own families, the number of adults who are not exactly related and who have their own family holiday traditions will grow incrementally. Talk about logistical nightmares. Take on the attitude of "the more the merrier" and everything will work out fine.

Guilt and Loyalty

Holidays can be brutal for the children of divorced parents. Kids often feel incomplete. If the children spend the time with you and your partner, they will no doubt feel torn about not being with poor Mom or Dad. Try to respect the fact the kids are thinking of their other biological parent and their nostalgia for the past is not a direct shot at you. It is nothing personal.

Virtually all kids have these fantasies, especially around the holidays. The kids like the idea of their parents together, even if in reality their parents cannot spend two minutes together in a room without making the children want to run off to the nearest closet and cry.

If the kids spend the holiday with their other biological parent, they will be missing your partner—and even you.

Special Days to You

Mother's Day, Father's Day, your birthday—there are lots of opportunities for feeling down about being a step-parent. But do not give in. An attitude will get you nothing but grief. Moping around because no one remembers your birthday is not fair. You have to tell people, "Hey, my birthday is on Friday and I want us to all go out to dinner." Tell your partner birthdays are important to you, and strongly suggest your partner talk to the kids about acknowledging it.

Mother's Day and Father's Day, "Hallmark" holidays or not, can feel like particularly high hurdles to cross, especially the first one. Do not leave it to chance. Discuss your feelings with your partner before you get disappointed. Then it is your partner's job to get the kids involved.

Before special events or days which are important to you, take the initiative:

- Be clear about your plans. Anticipate problems and discuss them with the children.
- Tell them your expectations. People are not mind readers. Talk with your partner.
- Do not expect a major deal about Mother's or Father's Day. The kids feel conflicted enough as it is. Acknowledging it is important, but celebrating it may be too painful.

- Yes, of course it hurts to be ignored or snubbed. Try to understand the positive intent behind it. It is not meant to hurt you. It is about guilt and loyalty to the other biological parent.

Gift Giving

Gift giving, whether for birthdays or holidays, can be another one of those step family expectation disasters. When it comes to step children and gifts, remember these points:

- You and your partner should discuss expectations and realities with the kids before the holidays. Financial matters may have changed. If children expect to receive many gifts, let them know ahead of time if things have changed.
- Do not expect anything from them. You can be pleased if the child whispers "Happy Birthday" and seems to mean it.
- Do not try to buy their love with expensive or large gifts. It will not make a difference in terms of how accepted you are, and it easily can cause resentment (from the child or from the ex-partners).
- Kids often cannot bring themselves to offer thanks to a step-parent. Give it time.
- A few children (step children or not) are rude and thoughtless. Others are simply blunt: "I hate yellow. Yellow is for babies." How you handle their rudeness is up to your partner and you, though I think it is vital your step children act graciously if your family gives them gifts.

It is easy to lose it when a step child looks up from the piles of loot and asks, "Is this all there is?" "Dad will get more for me." It pushes all your buttons. You are not caring enough, not rich enough, or she is not liked enough. It is vital you do not bite, because it is bait on the hook. Take a deep breath and say, "I hope you enjoy your presents. We chose things we thought you would especially enjoy this year." Let it go. Excuse yourself. Go to the bathroom and cry. Things will be better next year.

Coordinating Gifts with Others

Encourage your partner not to get into a one-upmanship situation with one partner topping the other's spending. You guys should be the model of restraint. Perhaps the ex-partner will follow suit. Often, reasonable behavior is met with reasonable behavior. Do not encourage your partner to buy joint gifts with the ex-partner. Coordination, conversation, and compromise only go so far and joint gift giving falsely signals reunification, and it tends to confuse kids by blurring family boundaries. Your family is your family; the ex-partner's is the ex-partner's.

The Destructive Power of Expectations

Let's review the destructive power of expectations. Because holidays are influenced with rituals, (and rituals are not considered rituals unless you do them over and over,) we all expect certain things to happen during the holidays. But what happens when the rituals change? We're still expecting them. If not careful, we will find ourselves back with the feelings of disappointment and pain.

The longer you are together as a family, the easier the holidays will feel as you develop your own rituals and traditions. But at first, the crunch of expectations and disappointment can make holidays rough. Each of you in your step family has an internal sense of what feels right for the holidays, and this sense is built from your past experiences. Every family does things slightly different, even if celebrating the same holidays.

Memories

And then there are the memories of how things were. Ah, memories of blissful childhood holidays when Mom and Dad were together and everyone was so happy. Things can get misty in retrospect. It is true, in some families, holidays are a time when people set aside their problems. But in others, people get depressed, get drunk, fight, and feel miserable. The holidays are the times of the year when people are most likely to commit suicide. For some families, it is the worst time of the year.

Despite this, children and adults alike feel nostalgic about the past, even when the past included unhappy family times. Kids want to hold on to their rituals, no matter what these rituals are. Rituals are part of who the children are. Many times, life is lived in the details, and it is the absence of the Christmas tree tinsel, or not having the dog around to sneak the turkey skin, which makes people most painfully aware there have been major changes in their lives.

Understanding and re-creating are not the same. There are times when it is inappropriate to try to re-create another's ritual. The loss of holiday rituals can cause a person to mourn, and it takes time—and maybe a few holidays without the ritual—to heal. Allow time for healing and do not try and force the children to get over their loss.

Weddings, Graduations, and Other Special Events

There are the times of celebration and rejoicing: family weddings, graduations, and your partner's parents' 50th wedding anniversary. But complications will arise. Who will host the graduation party, Mom and her partner or Dad and his? Can the two get along for a couple of hours? What about weddings? Who will stand up with the bride, her biological dad who she has seen two weeks a year since she was three, or her stepdad who taught her to ride a bike, how to swim, and solve math problems? If both the biological father and the stepfather are close to the bride, consider having them both walk the bride down the aisle. We are all adults and differences could be put aside for the happy occasion. Allow the bride to make the decision and stick with it.

You, the new step-parent, may be on informal trial, or at least close scrutiny. Everyone is watching to see what the exes do when the two see each other. What's to be done?

- Don't do the large family party and do a couple of smaller family parties. – OR -
- Do the large family party, and be the better person and welcome everyone to attend.

If your partner and the ex-partner can agree to disagree enough to negotiate who gets what event (he will do their son's baseball awards ceremony, and she will do their daughter's Girl Scout awards), the calm will help the children.

If there is harmony between the ex-partners (as there often is), relatives and friends of both people have a tough choice. Which one to invite? You and your partner may find yourselves excluded from other people's special events at times. It is tough deciding whom to exclude, and it is hard to cope when you are the one who hasn't been invited. The choice is often made not on a basis of whom the host likes better, but for other reasons. Try not to hate the host, and do not use the disappointment as an excuse to become hermits. Make sure to put the attention on the children and what is best for them. You can always drop the children off with the ex-partner at the party and ta-da – you have time alone.

Getting Help

Assessing the situation is the hardest part. Once you have made the decision to get help for your family, you will find there are lots of resources available. Therapy is a tool. It is a way to learn to take care of each of you, and heal old wounds. Therapy is positive. Because you are seeking therapy does not mean you are crazy, your family is a failure, or you have done anything wrong and need punishment.

When you have decided to get help, you may have to push the issue with the rest of the family. Because the family resists at first does not mean you should give up the idea without trying. Go by yourself for the first couple of times, if necessary.

Finding the Right Person

There are different types of therapies and types of therapists. When you are looking for a therapist or other mental health professional to help you and your family, you can begin by following these tips:

- Ask friends and family members.
- Check with local social service agencies, family service agencies, and the national agencies. All these can give you referrals to therapists in your area. In many parts of the country, mental health professionals advertise in local weekly or monthly papers. Search online for one near you.
- Check with your insurance company.

When you first call a mental health professional, you will spend the first few minutes on the phone briefly describing your family's problems and getting a sense if this is the right therapist for you. Do not feel shy about asking questions. In the normal course of therapy, you will not be asking questions about the therapist, get your initial questions out of the way now. Remember you are hiring the therapist, not vice versa. You have to be comfortable with them.

Here are a few suggestions of questions to ask:

- What's your training and experience? Credentials? (Credentials are explained later).
- What is your experience working with step families? You want someone who specializes or who has had experience in step family relationships. There are particular dynamics to step families, and you cannot use the therapeutic approaches, methods, or information you would for a nuclear family.
- Are you affiliated with national or local step family support systems?
- What are your rates? Do you have a sliding scale?
- How often do you generally meet with your clients? Will you meet with us individually, or primarily as a group?
- How will you evaluate my family's problems?
- How do you approach the problem I am seeking help for?
- Have you had success with short-term and long-term therapy?

Listen to how the therapist answers the questions and what is answered. Does the therapist seem to hear your family's situation, or jump to conclusions? You may need to talk to several people before you find one you are comfortable with. By having the right letters after a name does not mean the therapist scores well on the empathy, wisdom, and insight scales.

If all feels right on the phone, schedule an initial session. Keep an open mind. You may trust the therapist, but your partner and step children may not. Each person attending the therapy has to approve of the person. If you have a reluctant step child, you and your partner may need to put your foot down and insist he attends. Therapy builds a tight relationship between client and therapist.

What the Initials Mean

Mental health professionals vary in education. Here is a breakdown of what all those initials mean:

- Psychiatrist: Graduation from medical school, and then graduation from a psychiatric residency program. Some psychiatrists are also board certified, which requires them to take another competency. Keep in mind, here, unless the residency specifically focuses on psychotherapy, a psychiatrist can conceivably have no training or experience in it. Most physicians who practice psychotherapy, however, do pursue advanced training. The problem with this is the person likely received such training at a psychoanalytic institute. Such places vary widely in quality, and can be rather limited in their orientation. Among the practitioners discussed here, at present only psychiatrists can prescribe medication.

- Psychoanalyst: A psychoanalyst must complete training at an analytic institute. Sounds advanced but there are cautions. First, there are institutes and there are institutes. Second, many institutes accept candidates who have some or no prior background in the field. A few institutes will not even consider an applicant other than a medical doctor who, as discussed above, may have no background in psychology. Thus, the analyst's only training may be in an institute's possibly narrow view of the field.

- Psychologist: Ph.D. psychologists have about 5 years of graduate training in psychology and an undergraduate psychology degree. Psychologist D. psychologists have almost as much training but with less emphasis on the scientific aspects of the field. In order to obtain the license as a Psychologist, most states require further (one or two years) post-graduate supervised experience in the field. A Masters level psychologist cannot be licensed as a Psychologist, and has only about two years of graduate training. During Ph.D. training, students spend up to half their time in clinical settings -- mental health centers, psychiatric hospitals, schools, clinics -- and receive one-on-one supervision of their work.

- M.F.C.C. stands for marriage, family, and child counselor. To get this certification, the Therapist must earn a Master's degree and then counsel people for a number of hours under supervision. The Therapist must pass an oral and a written exam to become certified. Keep in mind not all M.F.C.C.s will have similar approaches.

- Social Worker: Two years of graduate training, perhaps an internship, and a year or two of supervised post-graduate work before obtaining the license. The requirements and titles vary by state. Be aware there are licensed and unlicensed social workers.

In New York, the two types of clinical social workers are LCSW (Licensed Clinical Social Worker) and LMSW (Licensed Master Social Worker), but only the first is considered a licensed clinical worker. The LMSW thus cannot practice unless under the supervision of a licensed clinical professional - psychologist, social worker, or psychiatrist.

- An intern is a candidate for a counseling degree who is completing her counseling hours, while using the license and under the supervision of a certified therapist.

Step Family Support Groups and Organizations

As the number of step families in this country has boomed, the types support services have too. As an alternative or an addition to private therapy, you and your family might be interested in checking out other step family support systems. See "Resources" for a list of support systems.

All About Custody

This is not legal advice and should not be taken as such. You need to know the laws and terminology in your state as they vary from state to state. Go to the courthouse law library and ask the librarian for the family law statutes. Or go online and search for the statutes involved with custody (parenting) and read them carefully. For example: Florida no longer utilizes the term custody. It is referred to now as Parental Responsibility and Time-Sharing.

"Parental Responsibility" refers to the decision-making authority a parent has of a minor child. "Time-Sharing" (visitation) refers to the right a parent has to have their minor child on specific days and times. "Shared Parental Responsibility" (joint custody) refers to an arrangement in which both the care and authority/decision making rights are shared by both parents equally.

What Is Custody?

When a child has two biological parents who live with each other, both parents are responsible for making choices: where the child will live, whether she goes to public or private school, and what to pack in her lunch box. However, say the parents split up, then who makes those choices about the child's life? The court determines which parent has the decision-making authority. There are times when both parents must agree on things. Other times the biological mother may have ultimate decision-making authority over school location, but the biological father has ultimate decision-making authority over religion. It is based per case and what the court deems is in the "best interest of the minor child".

The parent designated the primary residential parent will have the child reside in their home for the majority of the time.

If issued, one parent has sole custody (sole parental responsibility), meaning the parent has been awarded full legal and physical custody and decision-making authority. The parent who does not have sole custody has visitation, the right to spend time with the child without the authority to make decisions.

More and more, people are arranging for shared physical and legal custody, which means all the responsibilities, caretaking, and decisions about the child are shared.

Deciding on Custody/Parenting

Regardless of whether or not you can agree on custody issues, it is best to have an Attorney. If the two ex-lovebirds decide to go their separate ways and agree on custody issues, life's a breeze. Papers are filed and everyone is happy (as happy as one can be during this time in their life.) But if a complete agreement cannot be reached between them, then there are custody battles. Such battles can be expensive and emotionally trying for the parents, and can definitely take their toll on each child. If the exes can do one thing right in life, it would be to resolve custody issues amicably, or at least privately. Children have a hard time adjusting to the break-up and spending time with each parent separately. The child suffers terribly over custody battles, especially when the battles end up in court.

Is Custody Renegotiable?

Keep in mind no custody or visitation arrangement is final. A decision made, whether individually or by the Courts, can be changed or renegotiated if circumstances change. All custody decisions should be made with the best interests of the child in mind, and this criterion is used by all Courts. It is what most custody battles focus on. But how the Courts apply this best-interest clause varies widely. Policies and treatment of custody disputes vary from state to state and jurisdiction to jurisdiction, and continue to change and evolve.

Visitation a.k.a. Spending Time

When one biological parent is awarded sole custody (sole Parental Responsibility) of a child, the other biological parent is generally awarded visitation rights. Meaning he gets to visit with the child during specific days and times.

The terms and schedules of visitation can be determined by the parents and other times are determined by the court system, and there is great variation among them. The most typical schedule for parents who live near each other grants the noncustodial parent visitation every other weekend, from Friday to Sunday evening, and at least one night during the week. However, many local living parents have week-on and week-off schedules. When parents live a long way from each other, schedules like this may not work. Instead, the child may spend extensive time during summer and winter vacations.

Again, in Florida, the term "visitation" is no longer used in the Courts. Florida Statutes state you do not "visit" your children you spend "time" with them. Visitation is now referred to as Time-Sharing.

Please keep in mind visitation, like custody (parenting), can and will be changed as needs change, or if circumstances change

Medical Consent

Getting Permission

Being a step-parent means you have no official legal status and the medical community may or may not allow you to authorize medical treatment for your step child. And because, legally, step-parents have no authority, care providers have developed policies to deal with these issues.

Say you walk into Emergency with your step child, who is choking to death on a coin. Yes, the staff will treat him no matter who brings the child in, as delay would cause serious damage or death. And if you bring the child in with a broken arm, the staff will treat him at your request, though they may try to delay until they reach a biological parent. The hospital staff may not treat the child if he needs major surgery, at least until a biological parent can be located.

You can get around this system partially if you have your partner grant you power of attorney, or if your partner, and your partner's ex, has signed a form authorizing you to represent your partner when consenting to medical or dental procedures.

Power of attorney forms and medical consent forms vary in their language from state to state. You can get blank form at an office supply store, local hospitals or doctors' offices. Once you have completed the form, have an attorney review the form for accuracy. Have it notarized by a legal notary public. Most banks will provide this service for free, and it ensures the medical establishment treating your child it is indeed your signature on the form. You may want to carry copies of these notarized forms with you and file them with your pediatrician and local hospital.

See Appendix A for a sample Medical Release Form which can be given to the physician in charge. Both biological parents should agree to this form and sign the form (if available). Make sure to contact an attorney if you cannot get agreement from biological parent #2.

Child Support

As a stepparent, you have no legal obligation to support your step child unless you adopt the child, in which case, you are not a step anymore. Reality is far more complex, however. Child support and other financial decisions between your partner and your partner's ex-partner are major decisions, often determined during the divorce. Like custody (parenting) decisions, financial decisions can be altered and modified as situations change.

If your partner gets child support for your step children, your financial earnings should not alter the amount your partner gets. If, however, you are providing the larger amount of the support (food, shelter, and clothing), the ex-partner can make a case your partner now has a higher amount of income available to raise the children and might try to get child-support payments reduced. However, the laws vary from state to state. You must know your rights. I found in Florida it will never matter how much your spouse makes in determining child support payments. Spousal income is only looked at in regards to alimony modifications.

Child Support

If child support is part of your life, you will often find yourself deeply entwined in the financial life of your partner's ex-partner.

If the step children are of college age and are applying for financial aid (loans, grants, or scholarships), be aware the amount of parental contribution the colleges expect is often figured on the total household income. If you are concerned about the effect of your finances on your partner's child support or your step children's financial aid, consider signing an agreement to keep your finances separate. Consult with your Accountant to see what options are available to you.

No matter what, you are going to be affected by financial arrangements for your step children. Whether it is money coming in or going out of your household, you should be concerned.

How Much Child Support?

Your state may provide guidelines, such as tables, formulas, and other ways of determining who pays what and when. Child support is determined by:

- Income of both parents.
- Daycare costs for child or children (if applicable).
- Health insurance for child or children (if applicable).
- The number of overnights spent with each parent.

Deadbeats

Men aren't the only ones referred to as "deadbeats." There are deadbeat biological mothers too. All parents, whether male or female, have a legal and moral responsibility to care for their children financially.

Keep the points below in mind in the event you decide to withhold payment:

- Child support is not tied to custody or visitation arrangements. A parent is not allowed to withhold support payments, even if he disagrees with the ex-partner, or even if the ex-partner is out of line and forbids visitation.

- Withholding support only hurts the children. Neither party is allowed to withhold visitation for non-payment of child support or any other reason, unless it is deemed harmful to the child. If there is a visitation problem, your partner should go back to court to get the visitation enforced.
- A parent must support their children until they are of legal age and have graduated from High School (and this age varies by state), unless they are on active military duty, the child is legally declared emancipated, or the parent's rights and responsibilities are terminated.

Pay on Time

Ex-partners often fight over support checks, and lateness is a common complaint. As a stepparent, you will keep everyone's blood pressure lower if you do not interfere when support checks are late. Leave it up to your partner, and try not to interfere or complain too much.

When a parent does not pay the child-support payment on time, the overdue amount is called an arrearage. Arrearages will rarely be forgiven. In some states, interest will be added to the arrearage. If your partner cannot make a child support payment, get them to the courtroom immediately for an adjustment.

Late support checks are a form of emotional testing by the ex-partner. If the ex-partner hasn't fully disengaged from the relationship, he will test to see if his contributions still matter, if the family still cares.

Understanding why the checks might be late does not make it okay. If the ex-partner is chronically late with support checks or the checks stop coming, call your attorney or the local Child Support Enforcement Office. Being a deadbeat parent is highly illegal. If the custodial parent owes more than $1,000 in child support, the information may be reported to credit bureaus. Other consequences for a deadbeat parent may include blocking a driver's license or professional license renewal, suspending a passport, garnishing wages or tax refunds, taking lottery winnings, seizing property, finding him in contempt of court, or putting him in jail.

Child Support, a Taxing Issue

Child support is tax-free to the receiver, and it is not a deductible expense for the payee. Only one household can claim a child as a tax exemption each year. Some ex-partners trade off. Legally, the person who has custody of the child for the longest part of the year is eligible for the deduction unless the other parent pays more than 50 percent of the child's support. If you are taking a deduction for a noncustodial child, you will need an IRS claim form, and you will need the other parent's signature. Either way, the ex-partners will have to cooperate.

Step-Parent Adoption

Adoption is regulated by states, and there are significant differences between how things are done in, say, Florida and California. Fortunately for us, some things are the similar, and many general principles and concepts do not vary too much from place to place.

A biological child is one's birth child. Adoption is a legal process in which an adult becomes the legal parent of someone who is not their biological child. Relative adoption is adoption by a person related to the child by blood or marriage. Step-parent adoption is adoption of a marital partner's child.

Step-parent adoption is a form of relative adoption, which is adoption of a child by one who is related to the child by blood or marriage. Another common type of relative adoption is adoption by grandparents, but step-parent adoption is far more common. Legally, there is no difference between an adopted child and a biological child for consent, surnames, custody, child support, inheritance and property laws, incest, and criminal law.

In most adoptions, the relationship between the child and the biological parents is most likely terminated. In a step-parent adoption, only the noncustodial parent loses parental rights.

Why Adopt Your Step Child?

There are reasons why you should adopt a step child. In this country, people can choose to live with whomever they want, people can support anyone they want, and can love whomever they want. But there are other reasons why a step-parent might want to adopt a step child.

For some, it is a matter of protecting the child from legal complications around inheritance. For others, it is an attempt to give equal status to all children living in the household. Or the action itself may be a ritual of public commitment, like a wedding ceremony. For others, it is making legal what is already a reality, the commitment, and the actions of parenting, have taken place long before.

If your step child's other biological parent dies, you may want to solidify your legal relationship. Thus, ends the uncertainness. It is all settled— medical release, names, inheritance, and guardianship questions.

What happens if you haven't adopted your step child and your partner dies? As a step-parent, you have no legal relationship with your step child. Unless you adopt or are named guardian in advance, the court will appoint a guardian in such a circumstance. Your step child may be sent to live with biological relatives, and you may not be able to gain visitation or time-sharing rights. Of course, all this is true if the other biological parent has not died. If your partner dies, your step children automatically go to the noncustodial parent.

Here are other reasons to consider adopting your step child:

- If the other biological parent is living but has abused, neglected, or abandoned the kids, you, their biological parent, and the kids may want to sever this relationship.
- Adoption is a demonstration of affection and commitment. It not only makes a legal commitment; it is also highly symbolic because the child literally becomes your child. And it certainly

stops all those arguments beginning with, "You are not my dad! You cannot tell me what to do!"

- You may consider adoption if you have shared biological children and you want the step child to have status and rights indistinguishable from the other kids. Adoption also helps reduce sibling jealousy.

- Adoption is permanent. Adoption provides emotional security for the step child. Adoption says, "You are mine forever—I choose you."

Is it in the child's best interest to cut him off from his other biological parent? Step-parent adoption may leave the child with a sense of loss and guilt, especially if the biological parent has been involved in the child's life. Even when the parent is not around, adoption is a serious thing. This is the child's parent you are talking about.

When Not to Adopt

There are also reasons not to adopt your step child.

- Before you start proceedings to adopt a step child whose other biological parent is living, give deep consideration. Adoption is permanent and severs the relationship with the biological parent.

- Adoption cures nothing. Although it might ease sibling jealousies, it does not erase all of the tension around your house. Adoption will not automatically solidify your family.

- If there is a doubt about the health or longevity of your partnership, hold off on adoption. As you are aware, partnerships can break up, but your relationship as parent, whether it is biological or adoptive, does not end.

Legal Guardianship

A legal guardian is a person appointed by the court to care for a child's personal needs, including shelter, education, and medical care. A legal guardian is not a parent. Unlike in an adoption, the parents retain their rights and their financial responsibilities for the child.

If adoption is impossible, unfeasible, or undesirable, consider becoming your step child's legal guardian. A guardianship establishes a legal relationship between you and your step child, but the parents remain the parents. This option may work for you if you are a custodial step-parent. In this case, you will need the consent of the other biological parent, but you may face less resistance than if you were requesting consent for an adoption. If you decide to become your step child's legal guardian, consider acknowledging this important step in your relationship with a family ceremony.

Using Lawyers

Lawyers are essential for adoptions. If you are beginning the journey to step-parent adoption, you will need support and lots of information to get through the legal aspects. Make sure you ask how many adoption cases your lawyer has done and whether he specializes in family law. This is the most important thing you can do for yourself.

Getting Consent

If the other biological parent is still living, he must consent to the adoption unless parental rights are terminated. Consent procedures differ. In some states, the birth parent must sign a form in front of a social worker. In others, the birth parent must appear in court.

What if you cannot find the birth parent? Consult a Private Investigator. Unwed fathers (if never married) must be notified in most states and, in other states, must give consent to the adoption. In most states you will be allowed to publish in the local newspaper to find birth parents. By publishing in the newspaper, it states an action has been filed against a named person. If anyone knows the named person it instructs him to contact the Clerk of Courts. In Florida, it must run in the paper for six consecutive weeks.

Terminating Parental Rights

If you cannot get consent from a child's parent, you must go to court for a Termination of Parental Rights hearing. You are going to have to prove the parent has given up his parental rights to the child. The laws are inconsistent from state to state on this one, but generally the court decides on parental rights based on both the parent's previous behavior toward the child (abandonment, abuse, or neglect) and character concerns.

Here are representative conditions the court may consider:

- Abandonment. Has the parent maintained an active interest in the child's life? What if the parent hasn't supported the child but sends cards on a regular basis? In a few places you must prove the parent intended to abandon the child. In other places, the parent needs to have deserted the child for more than three months. Abandonment (as with all consent law) is decided by the court. "The court" means the judge you get and the state you live in. Judges and states vary widely. Make sure you do your research before you claim abandonment to find out how things are done in your state.

- Abuse and substantial neglect. The court may need to see the abuse or neglect was significant, and it happened more than once.
- Failure to support. Failure to support a child can be considered a condition only when the parent could pay but didn't. In other places, chronic underpaying makes parents eligible to lose their parental rights. Deadbeat parents who are reluctant to consent to an adoption have made deals to avoid having to pay their child support in arrearage (the amount of back child support owed). Florida Laws state in bold non-payment is not a valid reason for termination.
- Failure to protect. Neglecting to protect a child from known dangers is another condition which may cause a parent to lose parental rights.
- Character issues. Depravity, open and notorious adultery or fornication, habitual drunkenness, and drug addiction are all conditions considered as cause for a parent losing parental rights.

As you might imagine, court cases discussing these matters can be brutal for everyone concerned. Make sure you keep records of incidents. Include the date, time and what happened. Pictures are worth a thousand words.

Filing the Petition

After the child is eligible for adoption, you must file a petition with the adoption court. Your adoption petition (which your lawyer will help you draft) will supply this information:

1. Your name, address, age, date of marriage, and other details.
2. A description of the relationship between you and the child to be adopted.
3. The legal reason the birth parent's rights have been terminated. This is either because he gave consent, or is the result of your Termination of Parental Rights case.
4. A statement you, the adoptive parent, are the best person to adopt this child. (This is where you may include the length of time you and your step child have been living together.)
5. A statement the adoption is in the best interest of the child. You may need to justify this (your lawyer will advise you).

You (and your lawyer) will also include in your packet the consent forms (or the court order terminating parental rights) and the official name change request, if you are changing the child's surname.

Change Names?

In most states, you can change your name simply by using it in all aspects of your life. You can call yourself anything you want, unless it is rude or intentionally confusing, capitalizes on the name of a famous person, or is chosen with attempt to defraud. Even though your step child or adopted child can use any surname he wants, he may have trouble getting it accepted for medical, school, or other identification reasons. If the child has the biological father's last name, and the stepfather is the one adopting them, the child's last name must change. It is a simple process (especially during an adoption) to file a name change request with the court.

When the petition is filed, it may be a few months before your hearing. Adoptive step-parents sit back and wait until then; others decide to go ahead have themselves declared fit by taking and passing the home study and the waiting period.

Are You Fit?

Okay, you are physically fit, but are you legally fit to be a parent? In most adoptions, being declared fit, which includes a home study and waiting period, are part of the standard process.

Most step-parent adoptions skip this "fitness" step. In particular cases, especially in the case of second-parent adoptions or if your adoption is being contested, you will need to be declared a fit parent, and go through the home study process.

The Home Study

The need for a home study is determined by the situation, your state, and who lives in your household. Home studies and waiting periods are often waived if the adoption is uncontested and if it is you, your partner (the biological parent), and the child at home.

The home study is an investigation of your home life to verify you are fit to raise a child. It is conducted by a state agency or licensed social worker. If you are required to prove your fitness, the agency worker or social worker will tour your home and will ask you questions. She will then prepare a short report for the court, to be reviewed with your petition, name change request, etc. Many states do not require the home study to be submitted to the court, and then it is up to the agency or social worker to determine your fitness.

What questions are included in the home study?

- Is partnership stable?
- Do you have a criminal record?
- Are you healthy, both physical and mental?
- Is your financial situation stable?
- What is your lifestyle? They will prefer it be moderate.
- How many other children you have in the home and what are the sleeping arrangements?

This is not as rough as it all sounds. Besides the fact your life is under scrutiny, the home study is fairly easy. It is not an adversarial situation. The social worker is interested in creating, not foiling, adoptions, and the report written should reflect all the wonderful strengths you bring to the child's life.

The Waiting Period

There is a waiting period between the home study and the adoption hearing. In non-step-parent adoptions, the child begins to live with the adoptive parents, and visits are conducted by the adoption agency or by the state. In step-parent adoptions, this period is often waived.

The Adoption Hearing

The adoption hearing is routine and can be waived for step-parent adoptions. In this step, the judge reviews the adoption petition, the home study report, and the name change petition and then signs the papers. You will get your Final Decree of Adoption, and the child's name will be changed (if requested). You are now legally the parent. Congratulations!

Saved by Grace

You Have Help

Wouldn't it be great if we had "extra help" with step-parenting? Do you want someone to talk to and lean on in those uncertain times? I'm not just talking about a spouse. I'm talking about Jesus. He is there for you in good times and bad. All you have to do is reach out to Him. He is on your side.

If you are new to faith, I want to introduce you to our Savior. If you have been a Christian for a long time, I pray you will share this information with others.

I'm not starting from the beginning of time, but going to the root of how Jesus relates to step-parenting. Jesus was raised by Joseph, his stepdad. Certainly, the circumstances surrounding His birth were extraordinary. Being conceived by the Holy Spirit and born of a virgin certainly places His "stepfamily" situation in a category of its own. However, when you stop to think about it, the God of the universe allowed His one and only Son to be raised by someone who wasn't His "biological" father. (If you want to learn more about Jesus, read Matthew, Mark, Luke and John - chapters of the New Testament of the Bible. It's a great start!)

"For God so loved the world, that he gave his only Son, that whoever believes in Him should not perish but have eternal life. For God did not send his Son into the world to condemn the world, but in order that the world might be saved through him." John 3:16-17

Most of the major characters in the Old Testament were raised in homes with parent and step-parent combinations. Some came about when a parent married following the death of his/her first spouse, but most occurred when their father married more than one woman. In today's society a person is divorced or widowed between each marriage. Regardless of whether we are in the Old Testament or today's society, my guess is that you and the biblical characters share some of the same confusion emotions and problems.

The number of pitfalls facing a step-parent exceed normal parenting. The likelihood for frustration, rejection, anger and exhaustion are also greater. If you can begin your step-parenting journey with God's love, grace and compassion, and make prayer a part of your daily routine, you will navigate the potential disasters associated with step-parenting a lot easier.

Prayer

Most people think you have to be taught how to pray. I've heard people say you have to use big "Christian" type words, or words that sound funny like "thou." This is all not true. Prayer is like talking to your best friend. Once you tell your best friend what is going on, you would listen to them for advice, right? It's the same with God. You tell Him what is going on and what you need and He will respond. God may speak to you through others, through books, and/or through scripture. You just have to be opened to receiving. You might also want to have a journal on hand and write down what you hear. You may not hear an "audible voice," but whatever comes into your mind, write it down. I remember one time asking God why my divorce was so painful, then at that very moment, a character on the show I was watching said "having no relationship is better than having a bad relationship." Wow – sure answered my question!

Here is an example of how to pray:

- When talking to God, make sure you do so in a way that feels most comfortable to you.
- When writing to God, make sure to use pen and paper. Write in your journal daily to record your feelings and what you hear God telling you.
- It's ideal to find a quiet space to talk to God.
- Read your religious scripture if that is your source of faith.
- To talk to God, open up your heart.

There is no perfect time of day to pray. Many people take time with God in the morning when they first wake up. But He wants us to talk to him throughout the day. He knows what you are going through and He wants to hear from you. If you are a new Christian, this might feel a little strange at first, but trust me, the more you talk to God, the more comfortable you will become. Don't be afraid to ask other Christians to pray for you. Just don't expect them to do it all for you – you still have to do your part.

So, what types of things do you pray for? Patience comes to mind with step children (or any children), love, understanding, peace, guidance, wisdom, knowledge, things you want to change, etc. Ask God for the wisdom to handle your emotions better. If you are a child of God, then no matter how chaotic things are around you, God promises to offer wisdom as you mature through trials (see James 1:2-5). Attempt to respond to your situation with the fruit of the Spirit: love, joy, peace, patience, kindness, goodness, faithfulness, gentleness, and self-control.

(Galatians 5:22-23). Not always easy, I know, especially when dealing with children/teens. You'll find yourself feeling better about what you contribute to your home. Again, don't be afraid of prayer. It's just a private conversation between you and God.

Compassion, Grace and Mercy

Compassion is sympathetic pity and concern for the sufferings or misfortunes of others. So just what is grace? Common Christian teaching is that grace is unmerited mercy (favor) that God gave to humanity by sending his Son, Jesus Christ, to die on a cross, thus securing man's eternal salvation from sin. What is the difference between grace and mercy? Though often used interchangeably, "grace" and "mercy" differ in many ways. In a nutshell, they are two sides of the same coin. Grace is a gift we don't deserve, while mercy is not getting the punishment we deserve.

How do we show compassion and grace to others?

- Words. Be kind and gentle in what you say and how you say it.
- Look for needs and opportunities. Simple everyday kindnesses and actions often help in great ways.
- Let it go. Letting "stuff" go is one of the easiest ways to extend grace to others.
- Be there. Sometimes just lending an ear, not saying a word, will help someone.
- Forgive. Forgive others as our Lord has forgiven us.
- Learn to ask for forgiveness. If you make a mistake, which everyone does, learn to ask for forgiveness from the person you hurt.

- Watch the way you speak. Don't speak "at" or "down" to people, speak to people.
- Gratitude. Show gratitude in everything you do. Be thankful for what you have and where you are in your life.
- Take an interest in others. Did you know the sweetest thing you can say to someone is their name?

Whether you realize it or not, Jesus extends his grace and mercy to us every day. Each day is a gift to cherish. You were blessed with another family, even though at times it may not feel that way.

Forgiveness

It may be embarrassing at times to admit that you don't like your step kids, much less love them. Ask God to help you see them through his eyes. Remember we talked in an earlier chapter about loss and grieving? It's important to remember that hurt people…hurt people. You may love your step children differently from how you love your own biological children. The goal is to learn to care even if they never love you in return. Stepfamilies are complicated, which is why you often need to practice sacrificial love in order to survive. Jesus is capable of filling us with an attitude of compassion and grace. He longs to fill us with love for others as He loves us (Philippians 2:2-5).

"We love because He first loved us." 1 John 4:19

Every home should be filled with forgiveness, especially a blended family home. Remember children from divorced parents are put in a position they most times don't ask for. It takes time to learn about others and get along. No matter what you have done in your life, God has already forgiven you. Even if you think you have done the unthinkable, unforgiveable, God forgave you. You are accepted by God no matter what. We all sin and we all continually ask for forgiveness. Shouldn't we extend that forgiveness to those in our life that we love?

"Start children off in the way they should go; even when they are old they will not turn from it." Proverbs 22:6

Support

Parenting/step-parenting is hard, and having others around who can support us and our kids is invaluable. Parenting, like most things in life, is best done with the support of others. We weren't meant to carry the burden of raising kids all by ourselves. In a world of individualism, we are told that believers are family, and we are to love and respect others in the family, no matter their age. We can all look around and extend friendship to those in a different stage of life than we are, whether through offering a listening ear, teaching a new skill, or just spending time with them. It's one way to we support and love the family of believers around us.

If you are not yet involved in a local church, I highly recommend it. You may have to visit a few churches in the area to see what feels right to you. You want an "I'm home" feeling, and you will know when you have it. The church is a great support system for your family. Get the kids involved in a youth program. The more people they have supporting them, the better. Sign up for a women's or men's group. Get to know other parents. All parents, biological and step, go through trials and tribulations. We have lots of wins and losses, but through it all if you will remain faithful to our Lord and Savior, he will give you the strength and courage to endure.

"The LORD will guide you continually, giving you water when you are dry and restoring your strength. You will be like a well-watered garden, like an ever-flowing spring." Isaiah 58:11

Conclusion

Here we are, exhausted and thinking our brains are going to explode from all of the information received. No matter if you are the biological parent or the step-parent, the concepts have been the same throughout our study.

DO:
- Pray.
- Be yourself.
- Love and respect yourself and others.
- Get to know each other – slowly.
- Listen respectfully to one another.
- Discuss everything.
- Never keep emotions bottled up or hold grudges.
- Address conflict positively.
- Establish an open and nonjudgmental atmosphere.
- Do things and go places together.
- Show affection to one another comfortably.
- Have respect for everyone's personal space.
- Be flexible.
- Shed anger and bitterness.
- Be honest.
- Be patient.
- Keep your sense of humor.
- Learn to compromise.
- Be understanding.
- Love the children no matter what.

- Keep the spark in your marriage. Spend time together away from the children.
- Encourage a relationship between the children and their biological parent that is not living with them.
- Include the children in the moving details, decorating and home needs.
- Explain to the children (if of age to understand), the financial situation of the family.
- Establish core family values and rules and live by them.
- Make new memories.
- Have a rewards or discipline plan and make sure everyone is onboard.
- Show kindness, compassion, grace and mercy.
- Forgive one another.

DO NOT:
- Try and do everything alone. You have a savior just waiting to hear from you.
- Be intrusive (unless you think there is a problem which could escalate into a horrific event.)
- Judge.
- Criticize.
- Force the new relationship.
- Choose sides.
- Let the ex-partner be dependent on you.
- Keep the children from their biological parent (unless it is court ordered or in the best interest of the child.)
- Keep the children from their grandparents and their other grandparents.
- Keep the children from other extended family members.

- Fight with your partner, your ex-partner or their ex-partner in front of the children.
- Cancel on visiting or spending time with your child.
- Bad mouth the ex-partner or their family members.
- Try and buy their love.
- Take things personal.
- Withhold child support.

I hope you can take most of this and incorporate it into your life. I also hope this makes things easier for you and validates your feelings. Getting into a step family can be rewarding and will make for new adventures. As with every new adventure, hold on tight because there will be bumps along the way but the ride will be spectacular!

Resources

Although there are other resources on the internet and in your city, these are a few of the recognized resources for Step Families and Adoption. Feel free to perform an internet search to find more in your area. Please note: I have no affiliation with these agencies.

Step Family
National Association for the Advancement of Psychoanalysis. This organization can give you referrals to therapists in your area. Website: www.naap.org
Step Family Foundation. Website: www.stepfamily.org
National Step family Resource Center. Website: www.stepfamilies.info
Blended Families. Website: www.blended-families.com – Offers a Free Step-parenting Tips Newsletter.
Step Mom Magazine. Website: www.stepmommag.com - This is an online magazine which specifically addresses the unique challenges of being a stepmom.

Adopting
Adopting Organization. Website: www.adopting.org/adoptions/step family-resources.html
Adoption Resources. Website: www.adoptionresources.org

Legal
Utilize the search engine of your choice for your local courthouse to research the statutes in their law library.

Obtain a local family attorney or family estate attorney for questions on legal issues. Ask family or friends for a recommendation or contact your State Bar Association for Attorney referrals.

Financial

Obtain an Accountant or tax preparer for questions on taxing issues. Ask family or friends for a recommendation or contact the Internal Revenue Service at www.irs.gov.

Appendix A: Sample Medical Release Form

Medical Release Form

I, _____ (Parent/Guardian's Name)
hereby give permission for all medical and/or dental attention to be
administered to my child/children in the event of an accident, illness or
injury (emergency or non-emergency) under the direction of the
person(s) listed below, until such time as I may be contacted. This
permission includes, but is not limited to, the administration of first aid,
the use of an ambulance, and the administration of anesthesia and/or
surgery, under the recommendation of qualified medical personnel. I
also assume the responsibility for the payment of such treatment. This
release is effective for the period of one year from the date given below.
Child/Children Names:

_____

_____

_____

In an emergency, please contact me at: (____) _____-_____

(____) _____-_____

Or contact: _____

Relationship to Child: _____

Phone #'s: (____) _____-_____

(____) _____-_____

Primary Insurance Company: (name, policy & phone#)

_____

_____

Secondary Insurance Company: (name, policy & phone#)

_____

In case I cannot be reached, the following persons are designated to act on my behalf:

_____

_____

_____

_____

_____

_____

Physician (name & phone #):

_____

Dentist (name & phone #):

_____

List of Current Medications:

_____

_____

_____

_____

_____

_____

Known Allergies:

_____

_____

_____

_____

Primary Parent Signature:

_____

Secondary Parent Signature: (optional)

_____

Date: _____

Notarization:

On this _____ day of _____, _____,

      (Date)   (Month)   (Year)

_____, personally

appeared before me in

(Name of parent)

_____County (in the state of

_____), and in my presence, signed this

medical release form.

Name of Notary Official:

_____

Signature: _____

Commission Expires:

_____

Index

About the Author

MICHELE SFAKIANOS is a mother and grandmother living in Estero, Florida. In 1982, she received her AS Degree in Business Data Processing/Computer Programming. In 1993, she received her Associate in Science degree in Nursing from St. Petersburg Junior College, graduating with Honors. In 1999, Michele received her Bachelor of Science degree in Nursing from Florida International University, graduating with High Honors. In 2009, she received her Real Estate Sales Associate license. Michele has worked her way through the nursing areas including Medical/Surgical, Pediatrics, Oncology, Recruitment, and Nursing Informatics. Michele has been previously published in two Poetry Books and a Nursing Journal and is the author of 16 books. She is highly respected in her areas of expertise. Her years of experience as a Registered Nurse, Mother and Life Transformation Expert have given her the knowledge and wisdom to write her books.

www.ingramcontent.com/pod-product-compliance
Lightning Source LLC
LaVergne TN
LVHW051521080426
835509LV00017B/2141